Rare Gemstones

Chrome sphene

Vesuvianite

Moldavite

Diopside

Epidote

Diaspore

Sphene

Vesuvianite

Californite

Sphene

Sphalerite

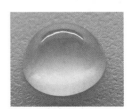

Prehnite

Apatite

Brazilianite

Andalusite

Sphalerite

Sphene

Danburite

Scapolite

Smithsonite

Aragonite

Fluorite

Scheelite

Calcite

Sphalerite

Calcite

Andalusite

Rhodochrosite

Rhodonite

Rhodochrosite

Rhodonite

Red beryl

Cobaltocalcite

Tugtupite

Rhodochrosite

Scapolite

Fluorite

Smithsonite

Diaspore

Danburite

All gemstones and photos on this page are courtesy of Coast-to-Coast Rarestones International.
Opposite page: Maw-sit-sit jewelry courtesy of Michael Sugarman. *Photo by Ralph Gabriner.*

RARE GEMSTONES

How to Identify, Evaluate and Care For Unusual Gems

Renée Newman

International Jewelry Publications

Los Angeles _____

This publication is designed to provide information in regard to the subject matter covered. It is sold with the understanding that the publisher and author are not engaged in rendering legal, financial, or other professional services. If legal or other expert assistance is required, the services of a competent professional should be sought. International Jewelry Publications and the author shall have neither liability nor responsibility to any person or entity with respect to any loss or damage caused or alleged to be caused directly or indirectly by the information contained in this book. All inquiries should be directed to:

International Jewelry Publications
P.O. Box 13384
Los Angeles, CA 90013-0384 USA

(Inquiries should be accompanied by a self-addressed, stamped envelope.)

Printed in Singapore

Library of Congress Cataloging-in-Publication Data

Newman, Renée.
Rare Gemstones: how to identify, evaluate and care for unusual gems / Renée Newman
p. cm.
Includes bibliographical references and index.
ISBN 978-0-929975-46-7 (alk. paper)
1. Precious stones. I. Title. II. Title: How to identify, evaluate, and care for unusual gems.
TS752.N495 2012
553.8--dc23

2011036093

Front cover photos:
Charoite pendant by Michael Sugarman. *Photo by Ralph Gabriner*
Sphene cut by J. L. White Fine Gemstones. *Photo by Jeff White.*
Seraphinite pendant by Carina Rossner. *Photo by Carina Rossner.*
Jeremejevite courtesy of The Arkenstone. *Photo courtesy Rob Lavinsky.*
Rainbow calcite (1865 ct, Balmat, New York) courtesy Coast-to-Coast Rarestones International. *Photo by Tino Hammid.*
Sphalerite courtesy of Pala International. *Photo by Mia Dixon.*
Zultanite ring by Erica Courtney. *Photo by Diamond Graphics.*

Spine: Red beryl bracelet by Cynthia Renée, Inc. *Photo by Robert Weldon.*

Back cover: Earrings by Carina Rossner. *Photo by Carina Rossner.*

Contents

Rare Gemstones Sometimes Used in Jewelry 95

How to Care for Rare & Unusual Gems 117

Where to Find a Jewelry Appraiser 125

Appendix 127

Bibliography 133

Index 136

Acknowledgments

I would like to express my appreciation to the following people for their contributions to *Rare Gemstones*:

Ernie and Regina Goldberger of the Josam Diamond Trading Corporation. This book could never have been written without the experience and knowledge I gained from working with them.

Mineralogist John S. White. He has edited the descriptions of the gems in *Rare Gemstones*. His recommendations and corrections have greatly improved this book.

John Bradshaw of Coast-to-Coast Rarestones. He has provided pricing information for the faceted gems discussed in this book and added much helpful content.

Mark Anderson, John Bradshaw, Gagan Choudhary, Paul Cory, Jim Fiebig, Si and Ann Frazier, Michael Gray, Henry A. Hänni, Miranda Hayes Schultz, Helen Serras-Herman, Don Hoover, Bill Larson, Rob Lavinsky, Glenn Lehrer, Steve Pederson, John Rhoads, Carina Rossner, J. Blue Sheppard, Elisabeth Strack, Simon Watt, John S. White, and Bear & Cara Williams. They have made valuable suggestions, corrections and comments regarding the portions of this book they examined. They are not responsible for any possible errors, nor do they necessarily endorse the material contained in this book.

Beads Direct, Dona Dirlam, Four Winds Gallery, Hubert Inc., Nevada Mineral & Book Company, New Era Gems, Jane Ramsey, Amy Kahn Russell, San Wai Gems & Jewellery, Stonesmith Jewelers and Timeless Gems. Their stones or jewelry have been used for some of the photographs.

A & A Jewelry Supply, Gordon Aatlo, Juan José Virgen Alatorre, Gilbert Albert, Eve Alfillé, Mark Anderson, The Arkenstone, Auction Market Resource, Bear Essentials, Gagan Choudhary, Coast-to-Coast Rarestones International, Columbia Gem House, Conchia, Erica Courtney, Paula Crevoshay, Cynthia Renée Inc, D & J Rare Gems, Dancing Designs, Tom DeGasperis, Devon Fine Jewelry, Diamond Graphics, Different Seasons Jewelry, Divina Pearls, Mia Dixon, Jessica Dow, Robert Drummond, Frédéric Duclos, Gary Dulac Goldsmith, John & Lydia Dyer, Lisa Elser, Mary Esses, Claudio Grage, Cristina Gregory, Gurhan, Henry A. Hänni, Yossi Harari, Helen Serras-Herman, Jeff & Lynn Hill, Hubert Inc, Iteco, Inc., Jamie Joseph Designs, Jone-Gems, Inc, Kothari, Richard Krementz Gemstones, Lang Antique & Estate Jewelry, Rob Lavinsky, Glenn Lehrer, Gail Levine, Mayer & Watt, Wimon Manorotkul, Heather B. Moore, Muse Imports, Nevada Mineral & Book Co, New Era Gems, Pala International, Pearce Design, Randy Polk Designs, Rainforest Design, Carina Rossner, Amy Kahn Russell, Susan Sadler, San Wai Gems & Jewellery, Andrew Sarosi, Tony Seideman, Sherris Cottier Shank, SSEF Swiss Gemological Institute, Philip Stephenson, Gerald Stockton, Michael Sugarman,

Timeless Gems, Geoffrey Watt, Barbara Westwood, Jeff White, John S. White, Bear Williams, Zava Mastercuts and Zultanite Gems LLC. Photos and/or diagrams from them have been reproduced in this book.

Frank Chen, Diana Jarrett, Dean Lange and Joyce Ng. They've provided technical assistance.

Louise Harris Berlin, editor of *Rare Gemstones*. Thanks to her, this book is easier to read and understand.

My sincere thanks to all of these contributors for their kindness and help.

Preface

Gems that were once only bought by collectors and rockhounds are now becoming increasingly popular in jewelry stores and designer boutiques. There are several reasons for this new trend. Jewelers and designers have discovered that non-traditional gems set them apart from their competition. Consumers want unique items to wear and give as gifts. New finds have made unusual gems more available for sale. Television shopping channels have done an excellent job educating the public about rare gems and creating an interest in them. Metaphysical practitioners and crystal healers have also generated enthusiasm for unusual natural minerals. The economy, too, has played an important role in the upsurge of non-traditional gemstones. Many of these gems offer attractive options to buyers who no longer can afford diamonds and gold.

In 1998, the first edition of my *Gemstone Buying Guide: How to evaluate, identify, select & care for colored gems* was published. It has been regularly updated since then. Meanwhile, readers who like my writing style and way of organizing gem information have asked for information on gems not included in that book. Rather than expand the *Gemstone Buying Guide* and increase the price, I decided to write a brand-new book focusing on rare and unusual gems; it is the first such guide on the market. *Rare Gemstones* is a companion to the *Gemstone Buying Guide.* All of the stones in this new book are different, except for red beryl and the gems on pages 132–140 of the *Gemstone Buying Guide.* Unlike my *Exotic Gems* series which explores rare gemstones in depth and devotes one or more chapters to a gem, *Rare Gemstones* is a more concise and general book like the *Gemstone Buying Guide.*

How the Gems Were Selected for This Book

In order to determine which gemstones to include in *Rare Gemstones,* I gave a long list of gems to dealers, jewelers and designers and asked them to mark the gems they had mounted in jewelry or thought were worth including. Some trade professionals also added gems. I then created a more selective list and tried to collect photos of those stones either loose or mounted in jewelry; the availability of the stones and photographs of them became important selection criteria. The gemstones I ultimately included are divided into two sections: "Rare Gems Used in Jewelry" and "Rare Gems Sometimes Used in Jewelry."

How This Book Differs from Other Gem Books

One of the distinguishing features of *Rare Gemstones* is that it provides general retail price ranges for the gems. These are based on a variety of sources including gem and mineral shows, jewelry stores, rock shops, Internet sellers, price lists, catalogues and consultations with gem dealers. Two or more trade members have read each section and checked the pricing and other technical information.

Another feature is that a high percentage of the photographs show the gems set in jewelry, rather than only loose. Finding jewelry photos is more challenging and time consuming, but it provides readers with design ideas and shows how stones believed to be only for collectors can also make attractive jewelry. A chapter on gem care offers ideas on how to prevent damage to fragile gemstones.

Rare Gemstones includes more information on quality evaluation than most other general gemstone guides (with the exception of its companion, the *Gemstone Buying Guide*, which contains seven chapters specifically on colored gem evaluation). If a gem identification guide does mention quality factors, it typically lists the four C's of color, clarity, cut and carat weight and states that color is always the most important factor for colored gemstones. I have found that with some stones such as chrysocolla, dumortierite and rhodochrosite, other value factors are just as important and sometimes more important than color. One of the most important price factors— transparency—is usually ignored in other books and simply lumped together with clarity, when it is in fact a distinct price factor, and a very important one. For example, the difference in price between an emerald with high transparency and one that is translucent can be thousands of dollars. Similar price differences can occur with highly translucent jade versus semi-opaque jade. In general, transparency is what can turn stones such as cuprite, diaspore, dumortierite, kyanite, rhodochrosite, rhodonite, sodalite and zoisite into gem-grade material.

Many gem identification guides exclude treatments from their gemstone discussions and descriptions. *Rare Gemstones* includes this information because enhancements play an important role in gem valuation. High-quality untreated gems are usually priced higher than treated stones. You'll find enhancement information in the list of gem properties preceding the descriptive text; when warranted, I've included more detailed treatment information within the text itself.

Rare Gemstones is unique because it focuses on rare and unusual gems. As a result, it provides more up-to-date information and photos of these stones than you will find in other general gemstone books. Researching the gems in this book has increased my admiration for the wide variety of minerals nature has to offer. Stones that never interested me before attract my attention now that I have learned how beautiful and intriguing they can be. I hope that after reading this book, you will have the same appreciation for these gems that I have gained while writing it.

Rare Gems Used in Jewelry

Andalusite (and a LOO site), silicates class; andalusite group
Chiastolite; a variety of andalusite
Chemical formula: Al_2SiO_5, aluminum silicate. Kyanite and sillimanite have the same chemical composition as andalusite, but different crystal structures.

RI: 1.63–1.65   **Cleavage**: good in one direction, poor in one direction
Birefringence: .007–.013   **Hardness**: 6.5–7.5; chiastolite 5–5.5
Luster: vitreous, greasy   **SG**: 3.13–3.20 (lower for chiastolite)
Dispersion: .016   **Optic char**: DR biaxial negative; chiastolite: AGG
Fracture: conchoidal   **Crystal system**: orthorhombic
Toughness: Fair to good   **Crystal shape**: slender prisms, waterworn pebbles, massive
Absorption spectrum: not diagnostic, but may show clusters of fine lines around 485 nm to 518 nm, and around 550 nm.
Pleochroism: strong with two or three pleochroic colors in green and orange stones---typically yellowish green, reddish brown, and yellow or green or colorless.
Fluorescence: inert to LW; may fluoresce weak to moderate green to yellowish green in SW.
Treatments: normally none. It can be heat treated to improve its color, but this is seldom done. Stable to light; stable to heat unless liquid inclusions are present; no reaction to chemicals. Ultrasonic cleaning is usually safe, steamer is risky if liquid inclusions are present.

Sometimes called the "poor man's alexandrite," andalusite often displays two distinct colors face up, which are usually yellowish green and orange. A third yellow color may also be visible. Unlike alexandrite, whose colors change when the lighting is switched from daylight to incandescent lighting, andalusite typically shows two colors simultaneously under the same light. This is because cutters generally orient andalusite to maximize its strong **pleochroism,** the property of certain minerals to exhibit different colors when viewed from different directions. The contrasting colors create a distinctive looking gemstone. Gem cuts with a long axis such as an oval or rectangle tend to show one color near the center and a second color near the ends; round cuts usually blend the colors into a mosaic. Occasionally, andalusites are cut to emphasize just their orange or pink color.

Fig. An.1 Andalusite. *Gem from D & J Rare Gems; photo by Donna Rhoads.*

Fig. An.2 Andalusite. *Gem and photo from Coast-to-Coast Rarestones International.*

Fig. An.3 Andalusite ring. *Design © by Eve J. Alfillé; photo by Matthew Arden.*

Fig. An.4 Andalusite ring. *Jewelry and photo by Timeless Gems.*

Andalusite is named after Andalusia, an autonomous community in Spain where it was first discovered. A translucent variety that has graphite inclusions forming a cross is called chiastolite. The name is from the Greek *chiastos,* meaning "arranged diagonally" because the pattern of carbon inclusions resembles the Greek letter *chi,* which is written "χ." Chiastolite is sometimes cut as amulets in countries such as Spain, where the symbol of the cross has deep religious significance. Because of impurities, chiastolite may have a lower hardness and density than transparent stones.

Fig. An.5 Chiastolite. *Slices and photo from Rob Lavinskty of The Arkenstone.*

Most gem-grade andalusite is from Brazil in the states of Minas Gerais and Espirito Santo. Sri Lanka and Myanmar are minor sources. Chiastolite is mined in China, South Australia, Spain, Siberia, Myanmar, Zimbabwe, and California, Pennsylvania and Maine in the U.S. In recent years, large quantities of excellent chiastolite have been coming from Hunan province, China.

Despite its rarity and unique appearance, prices of andalusite are relatively low. Retail prices for extra fine andalusite above five carats seldom surpass $500/ct. Low-quality material less than three carats may sell at prices below $20/ct. The retail range of eye-clean andalusite about one carat in size is roughly $50/ct–$300/ct.

According to dealer Simon Watt, the finest andalusite would be orange-brown and olive-green with flashes of pink, but preferences vary. The tone (lightness / darkness) and saturation (intensity) is more important than the actual hue (e.g., orange, yellow, green, pink, etc.). Very dark or very light stones generally cost less than more colorful ones in medium to medium-dark tones. Unlike gems such as sapphire, where pleochroism may be a negative factor, it is desirable for andalusite to display more than one color in the face-up position. Clarity and transparency are important factors that can determine whether a stone is industrial, commercial, or fine quality. Highly included material can sell for less than $5.00/ct. The quality of the cutting also affects price because good cutting requires more time and usually results in a greater loss of weight from the rough. But it is worth the additional cost because the result of proper cutting is greater brilliance and a better display of color.

Apatite (pronounced "AP uh tite"), phosphates class, apatite group.

Overall chemical formula: $Ca_5(PO_4)_3(OH,F,Cl)$

The formulae for three common species are: Hydroxylapatite - $Ca_5(PO_4)_3OH$;
Fluoroapatite - $Ca_5(PO_4)_3Fl$ and Chlorapatite - $Ca_5(PO_4)_3Cl$

RI: 1.63-1.655	**Cleavage**: imperfect in two directions
Hardness: 5	**Luster**: vitreous
SG: 3.13–3.23	**Optic char**: DR, uniaxial negative, aggregate
Birefringence: .002–.008	**Fracture**: conchoidal to uneven
Dispersion: .013	**Toughness**: fair
Crystal system: hexagonal	**Crystal shape**: hexagonal prisms, columnar, tabular plates, massive

Pleochroism: blue—strong blue and yellow to colorless, other colors—very weak to weak
Fluorescence: blue—blue to light blue (LW, SW); yellow—purplish pink (stronger in LW);
  green—greenish yellow (stronger in LW); violet—greenish yellow (LW), light purple (SW)
Absorption spectrum: 580 nm doublet common in yellow, colorless and chatoyant stones
Treatments: may be heated to improve color and transparency; coating has been reported in a
  few stones since 2011; fracture filling is possible.
Usually stable to light, but some pink may fade; heat may cause it to lose or change color;
attacked by sulfuric and hydrofluoric acid; ultrasonics are risky; avoid steamers.

The increased availability of neon green-blue apatite in Madagascar has sparked
more interest in apatite as a jewelry stone because it resembles highly prized Paraiba
tourmaline. Other colors of apatite—yellow, violet, pink, "asparagus" green, and rare
purple—are also appreciated. Though apatite is usually transparent or semi-transparent,
it may also be translucent, and sometimes it may display a cat's eye effect.

Fig. Ap.1 Blue-green apatite cut by J. L. White Fine Gemstones. *Photo by Jeff White.*

Fig. Ap.2 Purple apatite from Urucum Mine, Minas Gerais Brazil. *Rob Lavinsky of The Arkenstone.*

According to John Bradshaw of Coast-to-Coast Rarestones International, the retail
prices for the blue and blue-green apatite from Madagascar and violet and pink apatite
can range from $20/ct–$300/ct. The true purple apatites from Maine command the
highest prices per carat at around $150/ct–$1000/ct; sizes rarely exceed 5 carats. Green
stones, though very attractive, are slow sellers and generally sell for less, about
$20/ct–$120/ct; exceptional stones will command a higher price. Prices for colorless
and yellow are significantly less per carat, ranging from $15/ct–$80/ct. Cat's-eye apatite
can sell for $10/ct, but intense colors that are semi-transparent with good clarity and a
good eye can go as high as $60/ct.

Green apatite is sometimes heated to produce neon blue and blue-green stones. Yellow Mexican material can be heated to produce colorless stones, and Madagascar stones can be "overcooked" to get a colorless stone as well. In 2011, the Accredited Gemologists' Association (AGA) reported that nano-crystalline synthetic diamond coatings are now being used occasionally to coat apatite in order to improve surface wear and luster.

The name "apatite" is derived from the Greek *apatein* "to deceive" because it was confused with other minerals such as beryl and tourmaline. Even though apatite is rare as a gemstone, it is a common mineral found throughout the world, including Brazil, Mexico, Madagascar, Myanmar, Namibia, Pakistan, Russia, Afghanistan, India, Sri Lanka, Canada and the United States.

Apatite is an important industrial mineral. It's primarily used in the manufacture of fertilizer and is a main source of phosphorous. Apatite is also an important mineral from a biological standpoint. Apatite, which is also called hydroxylapatite—$Ca_5(PO_4)_3OH$—is the main component of tooth enamel and bone. Surgeons use the mineral as a filler to replace amputated bone or as a coating to promote the growth of bone into prosthetic implants. Some dental implants are also coated with it to help promote integration into bone tissue.

Fig. Ap.3 Apatite (9.14 ct) from Madagascar cut by John Dyer. *Photo by Lydia Dyer.*

Fig. Ap.4 Yellow apatite (4.35 ct) cut by J. L. White Fine Gemstones. *Photo by Jeff White.*

Fig. Ap.5 Tanzanian apatite cat's-eye from D & J Rare Gems. *Photo by Donna Rhoads.*

Fig. Ap.6 Apatite pendant. *Jewelry and photo by Gary Dulac Goldsmith.*

Fig. Ap.7 Apatite pendant. *Created & photographed by Devon Fine Jewelry.*

Fig. Ap.8 Apatite crystal pendant. *Created and photographed by Carina Rossner.*

Fig. Ap.9 Mexican apatite cut by Lisa Elser of Custom Cut Gems. *Photo by C. Tom Schlegel.*

Fig. Ap.10 Tanzanian apatite. *Rough and photo from New Era Gems.*

Fig. Ap.11 Madagascar cat's-eye apatite. *Gem & photo: Coast-to-Coast Rarestones International.*

Fig. Ap.12 Madagascar apatite (6.97 ct) carved by Sherris Cottier Shank. *Photo by Amy Balthrop.*

Aragonite (uh RAG oh nite), carbonates class, aragonite group
Chemical formula: $CaCO_3$, calcium carbonate, a **polymorph** of calcite, meaning it has the
same chemical composition but a different crystal structure.

RI: 1.525–1.685   **Cleavage**: distinct in one direction
Hardness: 3.5–4   **Luster**: vitreous to resinous to pearly
SG: 2.93–2.97   **Optic char**: DR, biaxial negative, aggregate
Birefringence: .155   **Fracture**: subconchoidal to splintery
Dispersion: .226   **Toughness**: fair to poor
Crystal system: orthorhombic   **Crystal shape**: twinned hexagonal prisms, needlelike crystals
Pleochroism: none   **Absorption spectrum**: not diagnostic
Fluorescence: inert to moderate, various colors, may phosphoresce to LW and SW.
Treatments: aragonite is occasionally waxed or oiled to improve the finish and durability; pearls
    may be bleached, irradiated, heated, dyed, filled or coated. Much ammolite (a gem composed
    of aragonite platelets; see below) is impregnated with an epoxy substance for durability.
Stable to light, converts to calcite when heated to about 400° C and loses iridescence; crackles
with high heat; effervesces in HCl acid; attacked by other acids; avoid ultrasonics and steamers.

Aragonite was named in 1797 after the place where
it was first identified, Molina de Aragón, Spain. Today,
most transparent faceted aragonites come from the
Czech Republic and are usually colorless to yellow.
Retail prices are roughly $15–$60/ct. Aragonite may
also be pink, white, orange, blue and brown and is
sometimes chatoyant. Translucent material is used for
cabochons, beads and carvings, which are normally
affordably priced by the piece or strand. Argentina,
Morocco, Italy, France, Namibia, Mexico, Bolivia, and
the USA are among additional sources for the stone.

Fig. Ar.1 Aragonite (Bilen Czech
Republic). *Coast-to-Coast Rarestones.*

Aragonite is an important component of pearls.
Pearl nacre is essentially brick-like layers of micro-
scopic aragonite platelets. Interference colors may result when light passes through the
layers. According to pearl researchers, including author of *Pearls* Elisabeth Strack, the
nacre that forms over a cultured pearl bead is nearly always composed of aragonite
platelets. The composition of a natural pearl is more complex because the core may
contain an organic protein substance called conchiolin
which is involved in the growth and binding of the
pearl. Calcite prisms usually form with the conchiolin.
The newest formation, i.e. outer layer, is composed
primarily of aragonite platelets called nacre. Generally
speaking, oyster shells tend to have the same structure
as that of a natural pearl, with a core of calcite prisms
and an overgrowth of aragonite platelets, the nacre that
corresponds to the mother-of-pearl layer in the shell.
However, the structure of pearls can vary to some extent
among different species.

Aragonite platelets are also the main component of
ammolite, a Canadian gem which has a beautiful iridescence showing combinations of red, orange, yellow,

Fig. Ar.2 Ammolite. *Pendant and
photo by Fred & Kate Pearce.*

green, purple and blue. Ammolite consists of the nacreous shell of the ancient marine mollusk for which it was named—ammonite. The iridescence of ammolite is superior to that of pearls because the enormous pressure of geological compaction of the ammonite mollusk shells made the aragonite tablets of their nacre thinner, creating better light interference. Ammolite is available in jewelry stores now and is priced by the piece based on the size and thickness of the ammolite and the intensity, rarity and number of its colors. In sum, aragonite provides us with a diverse selection of gem material. For more information on pearls and ammolite, consult Renée Newman's *Pearl Buying Guide* and *Exotic Gems: Volume 1.*

Fig. Ar.3 Aragonite pendant. *Created and photographed by Carina Rossner.*

Fig. Ar.4 Argentinian aragonite pendant. *Created & photographed by Carina Rossner.*

Fig. Ar.5 Aragonite (Molina de Aragon, Spain) with the typical reddish brown color of the locale. *Courtesy The Arkenstone.*

Fig. Ar.6 Aragonite from Tsumeb, Nambia. *Specimen and photo from Rob Lavinsky of The Arkenstone.*

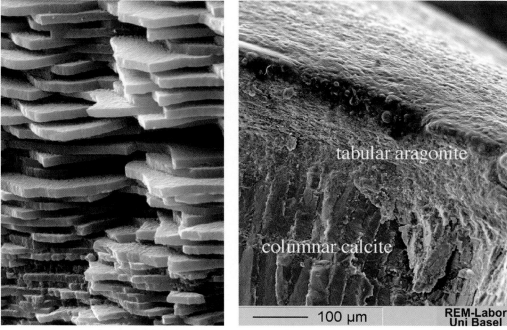

Figs. Ar.7 & 8 Left: Aragonite platelets of pearl nacre (approximately 5000 X). Right: Scanning electron microcopic photo showing tabular aragonite and columar calcite in a cross section of a natural pearl. *Photos © REM-Labor, Basel University; information from Henry A. Hänni.*

Aragonite is an important component of pearls and the mother-of-pearl layer of a nacreous shell. Pearl nacre is essentially brick-like layers of microscopic aragonite platelets. Interference colors may result when light passes through the layers. Unlike natural pearls, cultured akoya pearls consist primarily of aragonite platelets over a shell bead nucleus.

Fig. Ar.9 Cultured pearl necklace & nacreous shell from Divina Pearls. *Photo by Cristina Gregory.*

Azurite (AZH ur ite) carbonates class
Chemical formula: $Cu_3(CO_3)_2(OH)_2$, copper carbonate hydroxide

RI: 1.730-1.846	**Cleavage**: perfect to distinct in two directions
Hardness: 3.5–4	**Luster**: vitreous, waxy
SG: 3.70–3.89	**Optic char**: DR, biaxial positive, aggregate
Birefringence: .110	**Fracture**: conchoidal, uneven
Dispersion: weak	**Crystal system**: monoclinic
Toughness: poor	**Crystal shape**: tabular, prismatic, stalactitic, massive, crusts
Magnetism: strong	**Pleochroism**: moderate to strong: different tones of blue
Fluorescence: none	**Absorption spectrum**: not diagnostic

Treatments: may be impregnated with epoxy resins or paraffin to improve polish & hide cracks
Stable to light, but oxidation and weathering over the years may make it lose its deep blue color
or turn greenish; fuses easily, heat can cause it to break down and release water; attacked by
acids, effervesces with hydrochloric acid; avoid acids, ultrasonics and steam cleaners.

Azurite derives its name from the Persian *lazhward*, meaning "blue" in reference to its striking blue to violet color ranging from deep to light. It is usually translucent to semi-opaque, but it can also be transparent. However, faceted stones are often so dark in reflected light that they appear semi-opaque; in transmitted light, the blue color is mouth watering. Massive azurite used for ornamental purposes is also known as chessylite because of its occurrence in Chessy, France.

Fig. Az.1 A faceted azurite. *Coast-to-Coast Rarestones.*

Azurite has been used as a pigment for paint and dyes; however, the color is not stable over time. A unique characteristic of azurite is that it can gradually turn into malachite through oxidation. One reason for this is that the chemical formula for azurite—$Cu_3(CO_3)_2(OH)_2$—is similar to that of malachite—$Cu_2(CO_3)(OH)_2$. Because of malachite's ability to replace azurite through oxidation, the blue skies of some paintings from the Middle Ages that were colored with azurite pigments, now look green.

Most azurite on the market is intermixed with malachite, and is called **azurmalachite**, which is most often used for cabochons and ornamental objects. Solid blue azurite, though rare, is available as cabochons, druse and faceted stones. Faceted azurite generally retails for around $50/ct–$100/ct. Azurite druse and carvings are priced by the piece.

Azurite is found worldwide, but most transparent azurite comes from Namibia and Mexico. Other notable sources include France, Congo, Morocco, Australia, and the states of Utah, Arizona and New Mexico in the USA.

Fig. Az.2 Azurite on malachite (Milpillas Mine, Mexico). *The Arkenstone; photo:Joe Budd.*

Fig. Az.3 Azurite necklace by Gilbert Albert of Geneva, Switzerland. *Photo from Gilbert Albert.*

Fig. Az.4 Azurite from the Copper Queen Mine, Arizona. *Specimen & photo from Rob Lavinsky of The Arkenstone.*

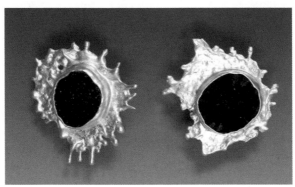

Fig. Az.5 Azurite earrings. *Created and photographed by Carina Rossner.*

Fig. Az.6 Azurite from Tsumeb, Nambia. *Specimen & photo from Rob Lavinsky of The Arkenstone.*

Fig. Az.7 Azurite from Chessy, Rhone, France, also called Chessylite. *Specimen & photo from Rob Lavinsky of The Arkenstone.*

Benitoite (be NEE toe ite), silicates class, benitoite group
Chemical formula: $BaTiSi_3O_9$, barium titanium silicate

RI: 1.757–1.804	**Cleavage**: poor in one direction
Hardness: 6–6.5	**Luster**: vitreous to subadamantine
SG: 3.61–3.69	**Optic char**: DR, uniaxial positive
Birefringence: .047	**Fracture**: conchoidal to uneven
Dispersion: .039–.046	**Pleochroism**: strong colorless and blue to violet-blue
Toughness: fair	**Absorption spectrum**: not diagnostic
Crystal system: hexagonal	**Crystal shape**: tabular pyramidal triangles or hexagons
Magnetism: nonmagnetic	**Fluorescence**: strong bright blue (SW), inert (LW)

Treatments: occasionally heated to turn it orange
Stable to light; sensitive to rapid changes in temperature; attacked by HF & concentrated HCl

Because of its attractive blue color, benitoite was thought to be sapphire when it was discovered in 1907 in San Benito County, California. Samples were sent for identification to the University of California Berkeley; experts there determined the stone were a new mineral. Benitoite's high brilliance and diamond-like dispersion (fire) have made it a popular gem among collectors. It is usually transparent and found in all shades of blue, but occasionally it is colorless, white, pink or greenish gray due to inclusions. Benitoite reacts strongly to short-wave ultraviolet light and fluoresces a bright blue color, which is useful for prospecting and locating specimens at the mine. Its dichroism is strong: the gem appears blue or colorless when viewed from different angles.

Benitoite has been found in Japan, but California is the only place where it has been mined commercially and found in gem-grade crystals. In 1985, benitoite was appropriately named the state gem of California. Unfortunately, commercial mining has ceased, and the gem is becoming increasingly difficult to find. Prices are high and on the rise. Stones above two carats are rare and can retail for as much as $10,000/ct, if you're able to find them. One- to two-carat stones may retail from $1000–$6000/ct depending on size and quality. For benitoites under one carat, retail prices are about $500–$2000/ct. Despite its rarity and high price, benitoite is sometimes mounted in jewelry, especially in central California.

Fig. Be.1 Benitoite jewelry from Paul Cory of Iteco Inc. *Photo by Jeff Scovil.*

Bixbite (BIX bite) also called **red beryl** (BARE ul), silicates class, beryl group
Chemical formula: $Be_3Al_2(SiO_3)_6$ beryllium aluminum silicate

RI: 1.564–1.574	**Cleavage**: indistinct
Hardness: 7.5–8	**Toughness**: good to poor, depending on clarity
SG: 2.66–2.70	**Optic char**: DR, uniaxial negative
Birefringence: .005–.009	**Fracture**: conchoidal to uneven
Dispersion: .014	**Pleochroism**: moderate to strong purplish red to red to orange-red
Crystal system: hexagonal	**Crystal shape**: flat-topped prisms
Luster: vitreous	**Fluorescence**: inert.

Spectrum: May show bands at 435 nm & 455 nm and broad absorption between 500 & 590 nm
Treatments: Assume that red beryl has been fracture filled unless otherwise stated because it is
　　typically heavily included and the filler helps mask the fractures
Stable to light; avoid heat, jeweler's torch, ultrasonics and chemicals, which may damage fillings

Red beryl (bixbite) is a rare intense red gem originally named after Maynard Bixby, the American mineral collector who discovered it in 1904. Since "bixbite" can be confused with the mineral "bixbyite," today it is normally called red beryl, although some vendors erroneously market it as "red emerald" (emerald is the green variety of the mineral beryl). Because of its rarity and rich red color, top quality red beryl has sold for as much as $20,000/ct. Commercial quality stones retail for roughly $800-$2000/ct whereas those of poor quality may be less than 100/ct. Most stones weigh less than two carats.

Fig. Be.4 Red beryl crystal from The Arkenstone.

　　The mining of red beryl is sporadic. The only commercial source has been the Ruby Violet Mine in the Wah Wah Mountains of Beaver Country, Utah. It has also been found in the Thomas Range of west central Utah, the Black Ridge of New Mexico and near San Luis Potosi in Mexico. More information about red beryl is available in *Gems & Gemology*, Winter 2003, pp 302–312.

Fig. Be.2 Red beryl bracelet by Cynthia Renée, Inc. *Photo by Harold & Erica Van Pelt.*

Fig. Be.3 Red beryl cut by John Dyer. *Photo by Lydia Dyer.*

Fig. Be.4 Red beryl (2.39 ct, untreated). *Carving and photo by Glenn Lehrer.*

Calcite (KAL site), carbonates class, calcite group
Chemical formula: $CaCO_3$, calcium carbonate

RI: 1.486–1.658   **Cleavage**: perfect in three directions
Hardness: 3   **Luster**: vitreous to greasy to pearly
SG: 2.58–2.75   **Optic char**: DR, uniaxial negative, aggregate
Birefringence: .172   **Fracture**: granular to uneven to splintery or conchoidal
Dispersion: .007   **Toughness**: poor in single crystals, good in aggregates
Crystal system: hexagonal   **Crystal shape**: spiky, tabular, butterfly twins, rhombohedrons
Pleochroism: none to weak   **Absorption spectrum**: any lines seen are due to impurities or dye
Fluorescence: may occur in various colors from strong to weak and is often patchy
Magnetism: most calcite colors—inert; cobaltocalcite—weak
Treatments: commonly impregnated with wax or plastic to improve polish appearance; occasionally irradiated to produce blue, yellow or lavender from white marble, but irradiated color may fade; calcite marble is commonly dyed and the dyes may fade.
Natural colors are usually stable to light; crackles at high temperatures; effervesces in many acids; avoid ultrasonics and steam cleaners

If you've ever taken a calcium carbonate supplement for your bones, you know what most calcite looks like. It's white and non-transparent. Calcite, which chemically is calcium carbonate, is often transparent to semi-transparent and colorless, yellow, orange, green, or blue. Clear colorless calcite is often called **Iceland spar** because when cleaved into fragments, it resembles ice, and it was originally found in this form at Eskifjord, Iceland. Today, most of it comes from Mexico. When several different calcite crystals grow together, and interpenetrate (a phenomenon termed **crystal twinning**), light passing from one crystal zone into another can be split into its spectral components. If the cutter orients the calcite properly, it may display rainbow-like colors; this material is called **rainbow calcite**. Calcite with multiple bands of orange, yellow, red, brown and white colors is a popular inexpensive material for beads, figurines, eggs, pyramids, bookends, table tops, lamps, vases, etc. It is sometimes erroneously called calcite onyx or Mexican onyx; however, it is not onyx, and some of the material sold as Mexican onyx is not from Mexico. Much of it is dyed. Banded calcite has also been sold as rainbow calcite.

Fig. Ca.1 Twinned calcite (Egremont, Cumberland, England). *Specimen from Rob Lavinsky of The Arkenstone; photo by Joe Budd.*

Fig. Ca.2 Rainbow calcite (Santa Eulalia, Chihuahua, Mexico). *Cut and photographed by Robert Drummond of Mountain Lily Gems.*

A rich purplish-pink calcite variety colored by cobalt is called **cobaltocalcite**. Technically it is named cobaltoan calcite and is $(Ca,Co)CO_3$. This mineral, found mainly in Spain, Morocco and the Congo, is sold in the form of druses, cabochons, faceted stones or mineral specimens.

Calcite is an important component of natural pearls and shells, which are used for carvings, cameos, beads and cabochons.

Calcite is inexpensive. Strands of beads can range from $1 to $40. Because of its perfect cleavage and low-hardness, calcite is difficult to facet; as a result, the prices of faceted calcites reflect more the difficulty of cutting than the inherent value of the material. Retail prices of fine faceted calcite tend to run from around $15–$50/ct depending on color and quality. Cobaltocalcite faceted stones are priced higher, as much as $200/ct because of their rare magenta color. Sizes are generally below five carats for cobaltocalcite whereas other calcites are available in sizes above 10 carats. Cobaltocalcite druses, which designers like to use in jewelry, are priced by the piece.

Even though calcite gems are not common, calcite is an abundant mineral found throughout the world. Industrially, it is used to make cement and to neutralize chemicals, soil and stomach acids. It is also a dietary supplement for people and animals such as cows. The world's most prestigious monuments and statues are composed of calcite.

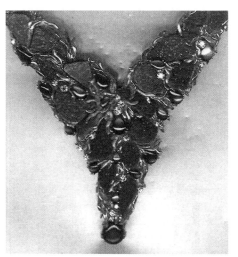

Fig.Ca.3 Cobaltocalcite necklace by Gilbert Albert of Geneva. *Photo courtesy Gilbert Albert.*

Fig. Ca.4 Carved cobaltocalcite. *Slide-pendant & photo: Helen Serras-Herman.*

Fig. Ca.5 Calcite and cobaltocalcite from Pala International. *Photo by Mia Dixon.*

Fig. Ca.6 Cobaltocalcite druse pendant. *Jewelry and photo by Carina Rossner.*

Fig. Ca.7 Shell cameo jewelry design by Claudia Lamboglia. *Cameo & photo: Rainforest Design®.*

Fig. Ca.8 Rainbow calcite (Faraday Mine, Ontario, Canada, 1,156 ct). *Coast-to-Coast Rarestones International.*

Fig. Ca.9 Cobaltocalcite druse pendant. *Jewelry and photo by Carina Rossner.*

Fig. Ca.10 Mexican calcite. *Cutting & photo by Robert Drummond of Mountain Lily Gems.*

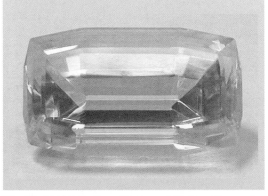

Fig. Ca.11 Calcite from Durango, Mexico. *Gem and photo from Coast-to-Coast Rarestones International.*

Fig. Ca.12 Latticework cameo carved from the Emperor (Queen) Helmet shell found in the Caribbean & beads of angel coral, another calcium carbonate gem material. *Necklace & photo: Rainforest Design*®.

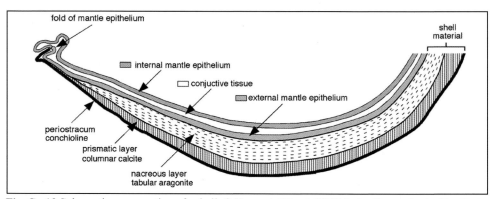

Fig. Ca.13 Schematic cross section of a shell. ©*Henry A. Hänni, SSEF Swiss Gemmological Institute.*

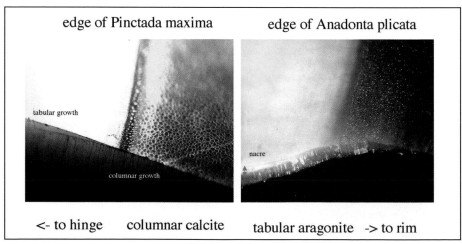

Fig. Ca.14 The construction of a shell (10x); transition zone from columnar to tabular structure. ©*Henry A. Hänni, SSEF Swiss Gemmological Institute.*

Charoite (CHAR oh ite), a rock composed of the mineral charoite, which is a calcium potassium silicate. The minerals aegurine-augite, K-feldspar and tinaksite are often included as components of charoite rock.

Cleavage: none	**RI**: 1.548–1.561 (for the mineral charoite)
Hardness: 5–6	**Luster**: vitreous, waxy
SG: 2.54–2.78	**Optic char**: aggregate if not opaque
Birefringence: .009	**Pleochroism**: colorless and rose-pink
Toughness: fair	**Absorption spectrum**: not diagnostic
Crystal system: monoclinic	**Crystal shape**: massive, fibrous
Fracture: splintery to granular	**Fluorescence**: inert to weak patchy red (LW); inert (SW)

Treatments: Commonly impregnated with wax or polymers to improve appearance & durability Stable to light, reaction to heat & chemicals undetermined; avoid ultrasonics; steamer is risky

Charoite is a beautiful purple, lavender and white variegated rock, which is used for beads, cabochons, figurines, carvings, vases, bowls, boxes, candlesticks and other decorative objects. It was probably discovered in the 1940's during extension work on the Trans-Siberian Railroad in the Chara River area of Russia; hence the name. However, it wasn't until 1978 that charoite was described and recognized as an independent mineral. Its only source to date is the Sakha Republic, Yakutia, Siberia. Attractive charoite cabochons are available for less than $100. Very large or exceptional pieces will cost more, particularly if mounted in designer jewelry. Charoite is used extensively as a decorative stone, but the supply appears to be dwindling.

Fig. C.1 Charoite pendant and cab from Nevada Minerals & Books. *Photo © Renée Newman.*

Fig. C.2 Charoite (131.51 ct) pendant by Michael Sugarman. *Photo: Ralph Gabriner.*

Fig. C.3 Charoite pendant. *Crafted and photographed by Carina Rossner.*

Chrysocolla (KRIS oh ko la), silicates class
Chemical formula: $CuSiO_3 + H_2O$, hydrated copper silicate

RI: 1.46-1.57, mean 1.50	**Luster**: vitreous, waxy, dull
Cleavage: none	**Hardness**: 2–4, rises to as high as 7 if intergrown with quartz
SG: 1.90–2.45	**Optic char**: DR, biaxial negative, aggregate
Birefringence: .023–.040	**Fracture**: conchoidal, sub-conchoidal, uneven, splintery
Dispersion: none	**Crystal system**: orthorhombic
Toughness: poor	**Crystal form**: botryoidal, massive, stalactitic, crusts, vein fillings
Fluorescence: none	**Pleochroism**: weak: colorless and pale blue-green

Treatments: may be waxed or impregnated with epoxy resins, plastic or other hardening agents
Stability to light: varies, some is stable, some might fade; heat sensitive; attacked by acids, rapidly by HF acid; porosity requires washing in pure distilled water, avoiding detergents, ammonia, etc.

Chrysocolla is a translucent to semi-opaque copper silicate, which is prized for its Caribbean blue and green colors. Its name comes from the Greek *chrysos* and *kolla* meaning "gold solder" in reference to greenish material that was used by the Greeks to solder gold. Many texts say the stone is unsuitable for jewelry if it has not been agatized with quartz, but chrysocolla can be stabilized with polymers and plastic substances to improve durability, as is the case with malachite, azurite, cuprite and other similar soft minerals. Crystal enthusiasts and some trade members, however, tend to prefer natural material.

The composition of chrysocolla is somewhat variable because of impurities such as silica, alumina, and manganese oxide. The more chalcedony (quartz and moganite) that's present, the more silicated the chrysocolla becomes, until it reaches a point where the chrysocolla is simply a stain agent. This material is called **gem silica chrysocolla** if it is translucent to semi-transparent and doesn't contain other minerals. Occasionally, it is simply called chrysocolla.

Over time, contact with the skin will oxidize a thin layer of the stone to a pleasant greenish blue color; when re-sanded and re-polished, the original color will return. Figure Ch.1 shows an example of a newly carved and polished gem silica chrysocolla piece next to one that has been worn for 25 years by the carver, Glenn Lehrer. Another interesting phenomenon is that gem silica chrysocolla sometimes has the ability to absorb water and dehydrate back and forth, depending on whether the stone is in a dry or humid place. For example, Lehrer noted that when he was on a plane to Bangkok, the piece would become cloudy and semi-opaque because of the very dry cabin air. However, after being exposed to Bangkok

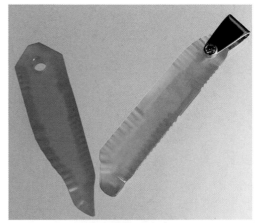

Fig. Ch.1 Newly carved chrysocolla (left) next to an oxidized stone that has been worn for 25 years by the carver, Glenn Lehrer. *Photo: Glenn Lehrer.*

humidity, the stone would revert back to its translucent to semi-transparent appearance. Some opals exhibit this same property and are called **hydrophane** opals.

Lehrer, a chrysocolla specialist and collector, says that the most valued chrysocolla is almost purely semi-transparent to translucent chalcedony silica with just a bit of chrysocolla present as the stain agent; it is free of inclusions, has an even color and is not hydrophane. Gem silica chrysocolla of this quality retails for around $200/ct– $300/ct and is very rare. However, you don't have to buy top grade material to enjoy chrysocolla. Prices extend to below $10/ct. Chrysocolla that is mottled and semi-opaque generally costs the least; cracks lower the price significantly. However, stones with interesting patterns and formations may command a premium and are used in designer jewelry. Such stones are priced by the piece.

If chrysocolla is mixed with other minerals such as cuprite, it is simply called chrysocolla and cuprite. One exception is **Eilat stone** which is a variegated blue and green mixture of copper minerals such as chrysocolla, malachite and turquoise from Eilat, Gulf of Aqaba, Red Sea. **Parrot-wing** is a mixture is of jasper and chrysocolla, which has a brownish green appearance. Chrysocolla mixed with quartz and other minerals is often called **chrysocolla quartz** and tends to be semi-opaque.

Chrysocolla is found wherever large copper deposits occur, but the most notable sources are Chile, Peru, the Congo, Mexico, Russia, Israel, and the Southwestern United States. The finest gem silica chrysocolla is from Arizona.

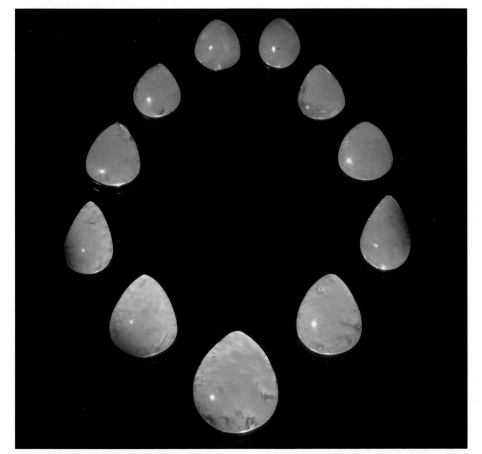

Fig. Ch.2 Gem silica chrysocolla suite from the Globe district in Arizona. *Gems from Pala International; photo by Jason Stephenson.*

Fig. Ch.3 Gem silica chrysocolla carving by Glenn Lehrer showing top transparency and a good deep saturation of the chrysocolla color. The green behind the clear chalcedony is silicated malachite. *Photo by Glenn Lehrer.*

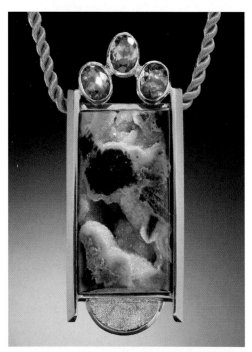

Fig. Ch.4 Chrysocolla druse pendant by Fred Pearce of Pearce Design. *Photo: Ralph Gabriner.*

Fig. Ch.5 Goddess pin/pendant by Paula Crevoshay featuring a chrysocolla gem silica carving by Glenn Lehrer. *Photo by Crevoshay Studio.*

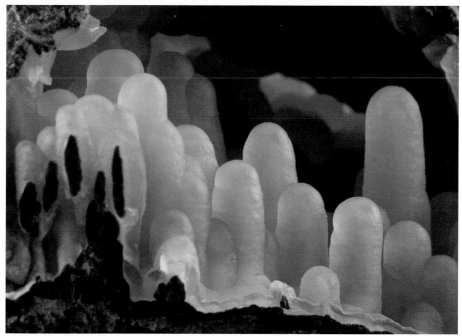

Fig. Ch.6 Chalcedony on chrysocolla stalagmites from the Inspiration Mine, Miami District, Gila Co., Arizona. *Specimen and photo from Rob Lavinsky of The Arkenstone.*

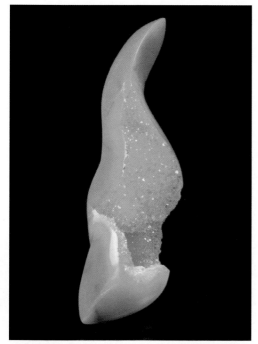

Fig. Ch.7 Chrysocolla druse from Globe/ Miami, AZ. *Pala International; photo by Mia Dixon.*

Fig. Ch.8 Pin/pendant by Paula Crevoshay featuring a chrysocolla gem silica carving by Glenn Lehrer. *Photo by Crevoshay Studio.*

Fig. Ch.9 Chrysocolla bracelet by Susan Sadler. *Photo by Jeffrey Mobley.*

Fig. Ch.10 Chrysocolla bracelet by Susan Sadler. *Photo by Jeffrey Mobley.*

Fig. Ch.11 Chrysocolla ring by Susan Sadler. *Photo by Jeffrey Mobley.*

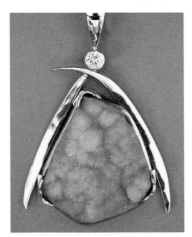

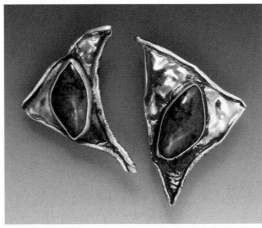

Fig. Ch.12 Chrysocolla druse. *Pendant and photo by Tom DeGasperis.*

Fig. Ch.13 Chrysocolla earrings. *Crafted and photographed by Carina Rossner.*

Danburite (DAN bur ite), silicates class
Chemical formula: $CaB_2(SiO_4)_2$, calcium borosilicate

RI: 1.630-1.639	**Cleavage**: poor in one direction
Hardness: 7–7.5	**Luster**: vitreous to greasy
SG: 2.97–3.03	**Optic char**: DR, biaxial positive/negative
Birefringence: .006	**Fracture**: uneven to subconchoidal
Dispersion: 016	**Crystal shape**: prismatic, slender prisms
Crystal system: orthorhombic	**Toughness**: good
Pleochroism: none	**Treatments**: irradiation (rare) intensifies the color

Fluorescence: inert to strong—light blue to blue-green (LW), weaker (SW), may phosphoresce red when heated. Spectrum: may show a doublet around 580 nm.
Stable to light; fuses under the jeweler's torch, very slowly attacked by HCl and HF acids
Ultrasonics and steamers are risky cleaning methods. Warm soapy water is safe.

    Named after Danbury, Connecticut where it was first reported in 1839, most danburite is colorless and has been mined in Mexico since the late 1950's. It is a bright, durable gemstone, usually of high clarity, that can be worn with anything and that is available in sizes as large as 15 carats or more.

    Mogok, Myanmar has produced attractive light to medium yellow danburite, but it is rare in today's market. Madagascar is the primary source of brownish yellow danburite. It tends to be a shade or more lighter than irradiated brownish yellow stones from Dalnegorsk, Russia, which started out as a colorless to light yellow. Irradiation intensifies their color. Tanzania has recently been producing small quantities of intense yellow, and is the only danburite locality that has an intense natural color, according to John Bradshaw of Coast to Coast Rarestones International. The downside is that it is rarely clean; needle inclusions are routinely seen. Bradshaw reports that retail pricing for danburite is as follows:

colorless....$15-$100/ct
irradiated Russian....$10-$40/ct
yellowish-brown.......$15-$100/ct
Tanzanian bright yellow....$60-$800/ct
Burmese.....too rare to give a range although an exceptional stone certainly could be in the $600/ct range. Pricing would be based on the quality of the individual stone.

Fig. Da.1 Tanzanian danburite (4.87 ct) cut by
J. L. White Fine Gemstones. *Photo: Jeff White.*

Fig. Da.2 Mexican danburite (4.43 ct) cut by
J. L. White Fine Gemstones. *Photo: Jeff White.*

Fig. Da.3 Russian danburite pendant from D & J Rare Gems. *Photo by Donna Rhoads.*

Fig. Da.4 Danburite ring design © by Eve J. Alfillé. *Photo by Matthew Arden.*

Fig. Da.5 Tanzanian danburite. *Gem and photo from Coast-to-Coast Rarestones Intl.*

Fig. Da.6 Madagascar danburite (2.82 ct). *Gem and photo from Coast-to-Coast Rarestones International.*

Fig. Da.12 Danburite (21.44 ct) cut by John Dyer. *Photo by Lydia Dyer.*

Fig. Da.11 Danburite from Momeik, Mogok, Myanmar. *Rob Lavinsky of The Arkenstone.*

Diaspore (DYE a spore), hydroxides class, diaspore group
Zultanite (ZUL ta nite) gem-grade, color-change variety of diaspore
Chemical formula: AlO(OH), aluminum oxide hydroxide

RI: 1.69–1.75	**Cleavage**: perfect in one direction
Hardness: 6.5–7	**SG**: 3.3–3.5; Turkish material: 3.39
Luster: vitreous	**Optic char**: DR biaxial positive
Birefringence: .048	**Fracture**: conchoidal
Dispersion: .022	**Crystal system**: orthorhombic
Magnetism: nonmagnetic	**Treatments**: Normally none, but fracture filling is possible

Crystal shape: elongated plates, acicular needles, massive, foliated
Fluorescence: Inert to long-wave radiation; weak yellow fluorescence to SW UV. Turkish stones fluoresce green in SW.
Absorption spectrum: Not diagnostic: Turkish stones show broad bands at 4710, 4630, 4540 and a sharp line at 7010, similar in position to those of green sapphire
Pleochroism: Moderate to strong— violet-blue, pale yellowish green, rose to dark red or tan
Stable to light; heat may cause it to crack or cleave; avoid acids; clean with warm, soapy water.

Diaspore, whose color ranges from light green to yellow, tan, gray or pinkish, was discovered in the Ural Mountains, Russia in 1801. Transparent color-change diaspore was found in the Aydin Mugla district, Turkey, in 1977. Some diaspore crystals have also been found in Hungary, Myanmar, Massachusetts, Pennsylvania's Chester County and at least a dozen other localities around the world, but Turkey is the only commercial source of color-change diaspore.

The name "zultanite" was introduced in 2005. That year Murat Akgun, a Turkish jeweler, acquired the rights to mine diaspore in Turkey. In order to distinguish it from low-grade, non-gem diaspore, Akgun then gave high-quality, color-change diaspore the name zultanite in honor of the Sultans who once ruled the Ottoman (Turkish) Empire.

Zultanite's colors are unique. It can change from pastel golden green in daylight or fluorescent light to a sparkling light gold under traditional light bulbs and to a muted purplish pink under candlelight or low wattage lighting. The larger the zultanite, the easier it is to see the multiple colors, which are natural—not the result of treatment. Zultanite is an expensive stone, which can cost hundreds of dollars per carat. The distinctness of the color change, the quality of the cut, color and size are key price factors.

Fig. Di.1 Visible pleochroism in twinned diaspore from Selcuk, Mugla Province, Turkey. Crystal from Rob Lavinsky of The Arkenstone. *Photo:Joe Budd.*

Designer cuts typically sell at a premium. Although diaspore often has eye-visible inclusions, gems sold as zultanite are generally eye-clean in order to enhance its image as a high-quality gemstone. According to Zultanite Gems LLC, their stones are cut with excellent proportions and finish with a yield of only about 2–3% of the rough. For more information on zultanite, see Chapter 6 in Renée Newman's *Exotic Gems: Volume 1.*

Fig. Di.2 Zultanites viewed in daylight. *Zultanite Gems LLC; photo by Jeff Scovil.*

Fig. Di.3 Zultanites viewed in incandescent light. *Zultanite Gems LLC; Jeff Scovil.*

Fig. Di.4 Zultanite earrings by Devon Fine Jewelry. *Photo by Tony Seideman.*

Fig. Di.5 Zultanite pendant by Devon Fine Jewelry. *Photo by Tony Seideman.*

Fig. Di.6 Zultanite ring. *Jewelry & photo by Gurhan.*

Fig. Di.7 Cat's-eye zultanite. *Gem and photo from Zultanite Gems LLC.*

Fig. Di.8 Zultanite necklace by Erica Courtney. *Photo by Diamond Graphics.*

Diopside (pronounced "dye OP side"), silicates class, pyroxene family
Chemical formula: $CaMgSi_2O_6$, calcium magnesium silicate

RI: 1.66-1.72 (spot usually 1.68)	**Cleavage**: perfect in two directions
Hardness: 5.5–6.5	**Luster**: vitreous to resinous
SG: 3.2–3.4	**Optic char**: DR, biaxial positive, aggregate
Birefringence: .024–.030	**Fracture:** conchoidal to uneven
Dispersion: weak	**Pleochroism**: weak to strong light and dark green
Crystal system: monoclinic	**Crystal shape**: prismatic, massive
Toughness: fair to poor	**Fluorescence**: green – green (LW), inert (SW)

Absorption spectrum: absorption band at 505 nm with bands also at 456 and 493 , chrome – 505, 508, 635, 655, 670 nm

Magnetism: Black star diopside – picks up; chrome diopside – weak to strong; yellow diopside and vanadium dioxide (mint green) – weak; violane – inert.

Treatments: Normally none except for possible fracture filling
Stable to light; fuses under jeweler's torch; attacked by HF acid; avoid ultrasonics & steamers

Diopside is typically green, and the variety colored by chromium, **chrome diopside**, is sometimes used as an emerald substitute. However, it may also be white, black, brown, gray, or colorless. A rare variety called **violane** is blue or violet and has been used for inlay and beads; Italy and Russia are sources. **Cat's-eye diopside** and **star diopside** are other varieties; the star normally has four rays, although it may also have six. Synthetic diopside is white and used as a glass-making raw material because it is free of the contaminants found in natural mineral sources.

Fig. Di.1 Chrome diopside cut by Lisa Elser of Custom Cut Gems. *Photo: C. Tom Schlegel.*

Fig. Di.2 Russian violane. *Gem and photo from Coast-to-Coast Rarestones Intl.*

Diopside was named in 1800 from the Greek words *di* meaning "two" and *opsis* meaning "view' which may be a reference to the two possible ways of orienting the crystal or the doubled image of its facets when viewed under magnification.

Most chrome diopside is mined in the Yakutia Republic in Siberia, and has become available in significant quantities in recent years, thanks to the liberalization of the economy there. Yakutia is also the source of most Russian diamonds. Chrome diopside is a mineral used to help locate diamond mines and is sometimes found as an inclusion inside diamonds. Therefore it is not surprising that it is also found around the diamond mines in South Africa. Other localities for transparent diopside include Tanzania, Pakistan, Madagascar, Austria, Brazil, Canada, and Afghanistan.

Most star diopside is mined in India and is usually black or blackish green or brown. Cat's-eye diopside mainly comes from India, but is also found in Myanmar and Australia.

Chrome diopside is the most expensive diopside variety. Large chrome diopsides tend to be overly dark so very fine, top-end chromes over one carat will retail for as much as $200/ct. Sub-carat chromes will top out at approximately $125/ct retail and go all the way down to $20/ct retail for commercial material. Star diopside is very affordable at prices of less than $5 per carat.

Fig. Di.3 Star diopside. *Gagan Choudhary, Gem Testing Laboratory, Jaipur, India.*

Fig. Di.4 Sri Lankan diopside from D & J Rare Gems. *Photo by Donna Rhoads.*

Fig. Di.5 Merelani, Tanzania mint green diopside. *Crystal and photo from New Era Gems.*

Fig. Di.6 Sri Lankan cat's-eye diopside from D & J Rare Gems. *Photo by Donna Rhoads.*

Fig. Di.7 Chrome diopside earrings design © by Eve J. Alfillé. *Photo: Matthew Arden.*

Fig. Di.8 Madagascar diopside. *Gem and photo from Coast-to-Coast Rarestones.*

Dumortierite (doo MORE tee er ite), silicates class
Chemical formula: $Al_7(SiO_4)_3(BO_3)O_3$ hydrous aluminum borosilicate

RI: 1.678–1.723 **Hardness**: 8–8.5, massive varieties 7
Luster: vitreous to dull **Optic char**: DR, biaxial negative, aggregate
SG: 3.26–3.41 **Crystal system**: orthorhombic
Birefringence: .015–0.37 **Pleochroism**: blue-black, blue, colorless; black, brown, red-brown
Fracture: fibrous **Absorption spectrum**: not diagnostic
Toughness: good **Crystal shape**: fibrous, massive, columnar, prismatic
Cleavage: distinct in one direction, good in one direction, none observed in massive material
Fluorescence: may fluoresce blue or white to shortwave
Treatments: normally none. Stable to light; not affected by acids

Most dumortierite is blue to violet and translucent to semi-opaque, but it is sometimes bluish green, pink, brown, or brownish red and in rare cases transparent. First found in the Rhône-Alps of France, it was identified in 1881 and named for the French paleontologist Eugene Dumortier.

Fig. Du.1 Dumortierite ear clips. © *Henry A. Hänni, SSEF Swiss Gemmological Institute.*

Today much of the material comes from Madagascar, Brazil, China, Sri Lanka, Namibia and the United States. Semi-opaque material is inexpensive and commonly used for beads, cabochons, carvings, figurines, eggs and other ornamental objects, which are typically priced by the piece. Cabs often retail for less than $10/ct. Transparent dumortierite, on the other hand, is very expensive because it is so rare. Even stones smaller than 0.25/ct may be priced above $1000/ct retail if you can find them for sale. Their hardness of 8–8.5 sets them apart from many other rare gems, which generally have a lower resistance to scratching and wear.

Many stones sold as dumortierite are actually quartz colored blue by dumortierite inclusions. The correct name for them is dumortierite quartz. Both dumortierite and dumortierite quartz are well suited for jewelry.

Fig. Du.2 A rare faceted dumortierite from Brazil, *Coast to Coast Rarestones.*

Fig. Du.3 Dumortierite brooch by Amy Kahn Russell. *Photo © Renée Newman.*

Enstatite (EN steh tite), silicates class, pyroxene family
Chemical formula: $Mg_2Si_2O_6$, magnesium silicate, member of the enstatite-ferrosilite series with **ferrosilite** $(FeMg)_2Si_2O_6$, iron magnesium silicate. Enstatite usually contains some iron in place of magnesium. When a significant amount of iron replaces magnesium, the mineral has been called **hypersthene** or **ferroan enstatite** in the past. **Bronzite** is a variety of enstatite with a submetallic luster.

RI: 1.66-1.75	**Hardness**: 5–6 (varies according to direction and cleavage)
SG: 3.2–3.5	**Cleavage**: distinct in two directions; parting
Birefringence: .008–.011	**Crystal system**: orthorhombic;
Dispersion: low	**Optic char**: DR; biaxial positive
Luster: vitreous to pearly	**Crystal shape**: prismatic, lamellar, water-worn pebbles
Fracture: uneven	**Absorption spectrum**: bands at 506 nm and 550 nm
Toughness: fair to poor	**Fluorescence**: none

Pleochroism: weak to strong green and yellowish green, or brown and yellow
Treatments: sometimes heated to intensify green; fracture filling is possible
Stable to light; slowly attacked by hydrofluoric acid; ultrasonics are risky

 Enstatite is a common component of volcanic rocks and meteorites and has an unusually high melting point allowing it to resist the jeweler's torch. As a result, the mineral's name is derived from the Greek word *enstates*, meaning "opponent" (of heat). In addition to being used for gems, enstatite has been used to line ovens and furnaces.

 The most common colors are green (usually olive) or brown, but it may also be, yellow, gray, black or colorless. If enstatite is colored by small amounts of chromium, its color may approach an emerald green. Such stones are called chrome enstatite and have been found in the diamond mines of South Africa. They are extremely rare and are the most highly valued. As the iron content of enstatite increases, so does its depth of color, density and RI. Enstatite ranges from transparent to semi-opaque and may exhibit chatoyancy or asterism with four or six rays. India is noted for its star and cat's-eye enstatites.

 Bronzite is an iron-rich variety of enstatite, known long before enstatite was first described by German mineralogist Gustov A. Kenngott in 1855. Bronzite is noted for its submetallic, bronzelike luster. It often has a fibrous structure, which may create a cat's-eye or star effect. Bronzite is found in India, Greenland, Canada, Norway, Austria, Brazil, China, Russia and the United States, and is typically cut as cabochons and beads or carved into ornamental objects. The cost of bronzite is low; it is either priced by the piece or at about $1 to $20 per carat. Designer pieces naturally cost much more than mass-produced jewelry.

Fig. En.1 Burmese enstatite crystal from Pala International. *Photo: John McLean.*

 Most high-quality transparent enstatite has come from Tanzania, Myanmar, South Africa, and Sri Lanka. It can retail for as much as $200 per carat. Other sources of enstatite include India, Canada, Brazil, Kenya, Australia, Germany, Austria and the United States. Good and commercial-quality transparent enstatite typically retails from about $20 to $100 per carat depending on size and quality. Most transparent enstatites are below five carats; larger stones are often too dark to be attractive. On the other hand, Indian star enstatites are much larger—as large as 50 carats or more.

Fig. En.2 Hypersthene pendant. *Created and photographed by Carina Rossner.*

Fig. En.3 Bronzite pendant. *Created & photographed by Carina Rossner.*

Fig. En.4 Sri Lankan enstatite. *Gem & photo from Coast-to-Coast Rarestones.*

Fig. En.5 Sri Lankan enstatite. *Gem and photo from Coast-to-Coast Rarestones International.*

Fig. En.6 Sri Lankan enstatite. *Gem and photo from Coast-to-Coast Rarestones International.*

Fig. En.7 Sri Lankan enstatite. *Gem and photo from Coast-to-Coast Rarestones International.*

Fig. En.8 Bronzite pendant by Frédéric Duclos. *Photo courtesy of Frédéric Duclos.*

Fig. En.9 Tanzanian enstatite (4.95 ct). *Cut and photographed by Robert Drummond of Mountain Lily Gems.*

Fig. En.10 Bronzite earrings by Frédéric Duclos. *Photo from Frédéric Duclos.*

Fig. En.11 Star enstatite from D & J Rare Gems. *Photo by Donna Rhoads.*

Fig. En.12 Cat's-eye enstatite from D & J Rare Gems. *Photo by Donna Rhoads.*

Fluorite (FLOOR ite), formerly called **fluorspar**; halides class, fluorite group
Chemical formula: CaF_2, calcium fluoride

RI: 1.43–1.44	**Cleavage**: perfect in four directions
Hardness: 4	**Luster**: vitreous, subvitreous
SG: 3.0–3.25	**Optic char**: SR, aggregate
Birefringence: none	**Fracture**: conchoidal, steplike, splintery
Dispersion: .007	**Pleochroism**: none
Crystal system: cubic	**Crystal shape**: cubes most common, octahedrons, massive
Toughness: poor	**Spectrum**: green—634, 610, 587, 445, 427, others not diagnostic

Luminescence: variable but often strong – typically blue but also purple, red, green, yellow or white under LW and with same or different color under SW; some is inert; may phosphoresce a third color; some fluorites are thermoluminescent, meaning they glow when heated.

Treatments: Sometimes irradiated to produce a violet color from colorless material; often impregnated with plastic or resin to strengthen it; commonly heat-treated to lighten dark blue or black fluorite to blue.

Irradiated fluorite often fades; some natural-color material may fade in long exposure to strong, hot light, particularly pink, red, green and purple fluorite; sensitive to heat; decomposed by sulfuric acid; avoid chemicals, jeweler's torch, ultrasonics, steamers and prolonged soaking.

It's no wonder that fluorite is a popular stone among collectors. It comes in a wide array of beautiful colors---purple, blue, violet, pink, yellow, orange, green, colorless—and banded combinations of these colors; its crystals are well-formed, and it fluoresces a variety of intense colors, In fact, the word "fluorescence" was derived from fluorite because it was one of the first fluorescent minerals ever observed. In rare cases, a variety called **chlorophane** shows a color change effect. The

Fig. Fl.1 Fluorite cabochons from Jone-Gems, Inc. *Photo © Renée Newman.*

name "fluorite" comes from the Latin *fluere,* which means "to flow," since it melts easily and is used as a flux in the smelting of metals. Fluorite is the standard reference point for the hardness measure of 4 on the Mohs scale.

Fig. Fl.2 Fluorites from Pala International. *Photo by Mia Dixon.*

Figs. Fl.3 & 4 Color-change fluorite (chlorophane variety): McHone Pegmatite, Spruce Pine, North Carolina) illuminated by fluorescent light (left) and tungsten light (right). *Rough and photos from Robert Drummond of Mountain Lily Gems.*

Figs. Fl.5 & 6 A color-shift Indian fluorite viewed in daylight (left) and in fiberoptic incandescent light (right). *Photos by Gagan Choudhary, Gem Testing Laboratory, Jaipur, India.*

In spite of its perfect cleavage and low hardness, fluorite has been used since antiquity for jewelry, carvings, seals, beads, and containers such as goblets, bowls and vases. Occasionally, fluorite cabochons are capped with clear quartz to prevent the stone from being scratched or damaged, but it is more common to impregnate fluorite with a plastic or epoxy resin to strengthen it. Faceted material is very affordable, with retail prices for many stones ranging from around $5/ct–$30/ct, depending on the size and quality. Most fluorites sell for less than $50/ct, but a few exceptional, clean stones may retail for as much as $200/ct or more, especially if they are from a rare location. Strong pink, orange or color-change stones command the highest prices.

Large fluorites are easy to find. The largest so far is 3965.30 carats, dark blue and from the Denton mine in Illinois. It was cut by Art Grant and is on display at the Smithsonian Institution in Washington, D.C.

Fluorite is found worldwide, but some of the most notable sources include England, the United States, China, Brazil, Canada, Mexico, Namibia, Russia, Thailand, Peru and South Africa.

Fluorite has many industrial uses: it is a flux in the manufacture of steel; it provides the non-stick surface of Teflon cookware; it is used to produce many fluorine based-chemicals such as hydrofluoric acid, it corrects chromatic aberration so synthetic fluorite is a component of high-end lenses for cameras, microscopes and binoculars; it's a source of the fluorine used for the fluoridation of water, it is a catalyst for the manufacture of high-octane fuels, it is the source of fluoride for toothpaste and, and it is used to make opalescent glass and glazed tiles.

A good source of additional information and photos on fluorite is *Fluorite: The Collector's Choice* by Lithographic, LLC.

Fig. Fl.7 Fluorite necklace and bracelet by Jane Ramsey. *Photo © Renée Newman.*

Fig. Fl.8 Fluorite from Gilgit, Pakistan. *Gem & photo from Coast-to-Coast Rarestones.*

Fig. Fl.9 Fluorite from Rogerly Mine, Cumberland, England. *Cut and photographed by Robert Drummond of Mountain Lily Gems.*

Fig. Fl.10 Fluorite from Brazil (5.79 ct). *Gem and photo from Coast-to-Coast Rarestones International.*

Fig. Fl.11 Fluorite from Kadipani, India (6.71 ct). *Cut and photographed by Robert Drummond of Mountain Lily Gems.*

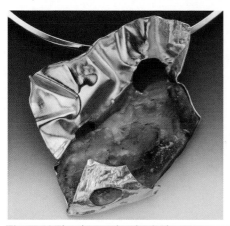

Fig. Fl.12 Fluorite pendant by Carina Rossner. *Photo by George Post.*

Fig. Fl..13 Fluorite necklace by Conchia® of Italy. *Photo courtesy creazioniconchia.*

Fig. Fl.14 Fluorite pendant by Heather B. Moore. *Photo courtesy Heather B. Moore.*

Fig. Fl.15 Carved fluorite. *Ring and photo by Gurhan.*

Fig. Fl.16 Irradiated fluorite (William Wise Mine, Westmoreland, New Hampshire). *Cut & photo by Robert Drummond of Mountain Lily Gems.*

Fig. Fl.17 Color-change chlorophane from North Carolina in tungston light. *Cut & photographed by Robert Drummond of Mountain Lily Gems.*

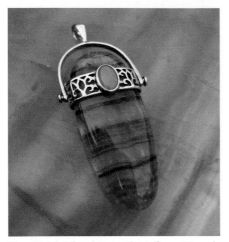

Fig. Fl.18 Fluorite pendant from Nevada Mineral & Book Co. *Photo © Renée Newman.*

Fig. Fl.19 Fluorite earrings from Nevada Mineral & Book Co. *Photo © Renée Newman.*

Fig. Fl.20 Fluorite (Mount Chamonix, France) on smoky quartz. *Rob Lavinsky, The Arkenstone.*

Fig. Fl.21 Fluorite (Dalnegorsk, Russia). *Specimen and photo from Rob Lavinsky of The Arkenstone.*

Fig. Fl.22 Fluorite (Illinois, USA). *Courtesy Coast-to-Caast Rarestones International.*

Fig. Fl.23 Fluorite (Okorusu Mine, Namibia). *Specimen & photo: Rob Lavinsky, The Arkenstone.*

Gaspéite or **Gaspeite** (gas PAY ite), carbonates class, calcite group
Chemical formula: $(Ni,Mg,Ca,Fe)CO_3$, nickel, magnesium, calcium, iron carbonate

RI: 1.61–1.83　　　　　　　　**Cleavage**: perfect in three directions
Hardness: 4.5–5　　　　　　　**Luster**: vitreous, dull
SG: 3.21–3.70　　　　　　　　**Optic char**: DR, uniaxial negative, aggregate
Birefringence: .220　　　　　　**Crystal system**: hexagonal or hexagonal-trigonal
Magnetism: strong　　　　　　**Toughness**: fair to poor
Fracture: uneven　　　　　　　**Crystal shape**: rhombohedral, massive
Effervesces slightly in HCl　　**Treatment**: may be impregnated with a polymer, wax or plastic

Accepted as a separate mineral in 1966, gaspéite was named after the Gaspé Peninsula in Quebec, Canada, where it was discovered around nickel sulfide deposits. It's a translucent to semi-opaque, yellowish-green stone that often contains brown inclusions. Recent finds in Australia north of Perth have increased its availability. Today, it is not uncommon to go into a specialty store, Indian shop or Southwestern US designer gallery and see gaspéite mounted in silver jewelry, strung as beads or cut as figurines. Sometimes it is set with turquoise, sugilite, lapis, opal and/or coral. Prices are relatively low and similar to those of turquoise; you should be able to find a nice cabochon for less than $100 retail. Faceted gaspéites are rare and range around $20/ct–$30/ct.

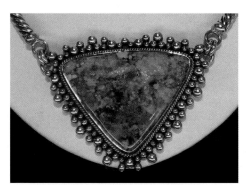

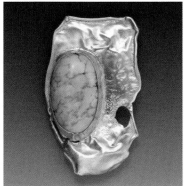

Fig. Ga.1 Gaspéite necklace from Four Winds Gallery. *Photo © Renée Newman.*

Fig. Ga.2 Gaspéite pendant. *Created & photographed by Carina Rossner.*

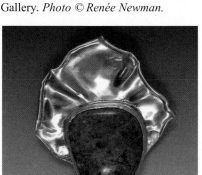

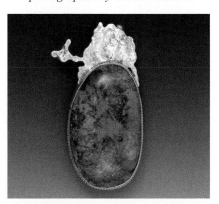

Fig. Ga.3 Gaspéite pendant. *Created and photographed by Carina Rossner.*

Fig. Ga.4 Gaspéite pendant. *Created and photographed by Carina Rossner.*

Hematite (HEM uh tite), oxides class, hematite group
Chemical formula: Fe_2O_3, iron oxide

RI: 2.94–3.22	**Luster**: metallic, sub-metallic, dull
Hardness: 5.5–6.5	**Fracture**: splintery, granular or subconchoidal
SG: 5.00–5.28	**Optic char**: DR, opaque
Birefringence: .280	**Absorption spectrum:** not diagnostic
Cleavage: none	**Toughness**: good to excellent
Crystal system: trigonal	**Crystal shape**: tabular, massive, botryoidal twins, thin plates
Fluorescence: inert	**Treatments**: normally not treated

Magnetism: non-magnetic, except if heated or intergrown with magnetic minerals
Stable to light; high heat may make it magnetic; soluble in HCl acid; ultrasonic cleaning is safe.

If you facet hematite, it resembles a black diamond because of its bright luster, opaqueness and dark gray to black color, but if you grind hematite, it turns into a rust-red powder, which was used as a pigment for Egyptian cave paintings, American Indian face paint and American barns. No other black mineral forms red powder or a red streak if you scratch it. Though still utilized as a red pigment, hematite's most important use is as an ore of iron. The mineral derived its name from the Greek *haimatites*, meaning "bloodlike," in reference to the red color of its powder. Hematite inclusions may be found in quartz or sunstone (feldspar), sometimes giving it a reddish color and/or creating a sparkly optical illusion called aventurescence. Some hematite is iridescent and is called rainbow hematite or specularite. Hematite druses are common.

In ancient times, hematite was cut and carved as seals, talismans, cameos and intaglios. It is still an important lapidary material for pendants, rings, bracelets and cuff-links; and hematite beads have been used to simulate black pearls. Because of its high density, it is heavy for earrings. Hematite is inexpensive and usually priced like costume jewelry except when it is hand-carved and mounted with gemstones in designer jewelry. Despite its low cost, imitation hematite is also marketed. One type is **hematine**, a magnetic man-made simulant.

The Lake Superior region of North America has been a prime source of hematite, but major deposits are also found in Brazil, England, Scotland, Italy, South Africa, India, China, the Ukraine and Australia.

Fig. He.1 Hematite cuff links from Lang Antiques & Estate Jewelry. *Photo courtesy Lang Antiques.*

Fig. He.2 Hematite. *Earrings and photo from Lang Antiques & Estate Jewelry.*

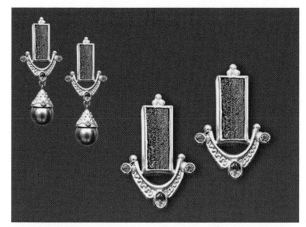

Fig. He3 Rainbow hematite earrings design © Eve J. Alfillé. *Photo by Matthew Arden.*

Fig. He.4 Botryoidal hematite. *Pendant & photo from Jamie Joseph Co.*

Figs. He.5 & 6 Hematite jewelry photos from Gail Levine's www.AuctionMarketResource.com.
Left: Hematite earrings, Weschler's auction 4-12-2006, hammer price $1,440.00.
Right: Hematite cuff links, Bonhams & Butterfields–NY auction 6-23-2009, hammer price $2,074.00.

Fig. He.7 Hematite ring. *Jewelry & photo by Gurhan.*

Fig. He.8 Hematite (Wessels Mine, South Africa). *Courtesy of Rob Lavinsky of The Arkenstone.*

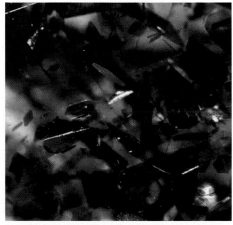

Fig. He.9 Randomly oriented hematite platelets in a Tanzanian sunstone from Pala International. *Photo by Wimon Manorotkul.*

Howlite, (HOW lite) a mineral species, which is a member of the silicate class $Ca_2B_5SiO_9(OH)_5$, hydrated calcium borosilicate

RI: 1.583–1.608 (spot usually 1.59)	**Cleavage**: none
Hardness: 2.5–3.5	**Luster**: vitreous, subvitreous
SG: 2.45–2.71	**Optic char**: DR, aggregate
Birefringence: .019–.020	**Fracture**: granular
Dispersion: none	**Crystal system**: monoclinic
Toughness: fair	**Absorption spectrum**: not diagnostic
Pleochroism: none	**Treatments**: dyeing and impregnation

Crystal shape: massive, compact nodules resembling cauliflower heads
Fluorescence: inert to moderate orange (LW); brownish yellow (LW)
Stable to light; fusible under jeweler's torch; dissolves in HCl acid; avoid ultrasonics.

Best known as a turquoise simulant, howlite is a translucent to semi-opaque white mineral that typically has a spiderweb-like black veining. Its porosity allows it to accept dye readily, making it an ideal material for imitating turquoise, lapis lazuli, coral, and red jasper. It was named in 1868 for Canadian geologist Henry How, who discovered it in Nova Scotia.

Southern California is the primary source of howlite, but it is also found in Nevada, Mexico, Eastern Canada, Germany, Russia and Turkey. Material found in Nevada is sometimes sold as "white buffalo stone," or erroneously as "white turquoise."

Initially used for carvings and backgrounds for paintings, howlite is now used for beads and cabochons. Mass-produced pieces are low-priced, with cabs selling on the Internet for as little as $1 and strands as low as $5. Expect to pay a lot more for better quality material and howlite mounted in designer jewelry. Natural-color howlite pieces coordinate well with black and white color schemes.

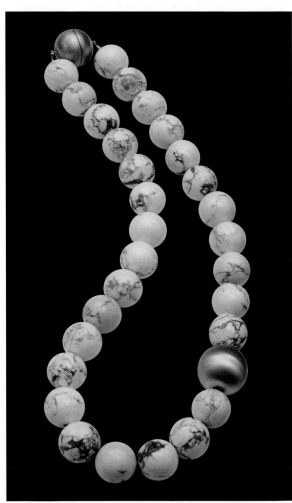

Fig. Ho.1 Howlite necklace by Frédéric Duclos. *Photo from Frédéric Duclos.*

Fig. Ho.2 Howlite and black onyx jewelry from Stonesmith Jewelers. *Photo © Renée Newman.*

Fig. Ho.3 Howlite bracelet by Susan Sadler. *Photo by Jeffrey Mobley.*

Fig. Ho.4 Howlite bracelet by Frédéric Duclos. *Photo courtesy Frédéric Duclos.*

Kyanite (KYE a nite), silicates class
Chemical formula: Al_2SiO_5, aluminum silicate, the same chemical composition as andalusite and sillimanite, but with different crystal structures

RI: 1.710–1.734	**Cleavage**: perfect in 1 direction, distinct in 1 direction, parting
Luster: vitreous	**Hardness**: 4–5 in one direction, 6–7.5 at approx 90° to it (GIA)
SG: 3.53–3.70	**Optic char**: DR biaxial positive or negative
Birefringence: .012–.033	**Fracture**: uneven, splintery
Dispersion: .020	**Pleochroism**: moderate; usually dark blue, colorless, violet-blue
Crystal system: triclinic	**Crystal form**: columnar, bladed, tabular, flattened, elongated
Toughness: fair–poor	**Magnetism**: blue & orange kyanite: inert; green kyanite: weak

Absorption spectrum: often shows iron bands at 435 nm and 445 nm in the violet. Stones that contain chromium might show faint, fine lines at 652 nm, 671 nm, and 689 nm in the red. Orange manganese-rich stones show broad band around 460 nm.
Fluorescence: Some kyanite shows weak red fluorescence under LW.
Treatments: normally none, but some material is heated and fracture filling is possible.
Stable to light; very sensitive to heat; not attacked by acids; clean with warm soapy water.

If you like sapphire and tanzanite, then you'll enjoy kyanite because it has similar colors. In fact, kyanite is occasionally found in parcels of sapphires. Its name is derived from the Greek *kyanos,* meaning "blue." The long, straight, pronounced color banding (most typical of the blue variety) is one of the best identifiers to separate kyanite from similar-looking materials, like sapphire, says Cara Williams of Stone Group Labs. This is particularly evident in the material that most resembles fine sapphire. It is also a good indicator of the hardness directions, with the softest direction perpendicular to the banding direction and the hardest along it. This color banding also follows one of the optic axes.

According to cutter Robert Drummond of Mountain Lily Gems, cutting parallel to the long axis of a kyanite crystal is much like cutting fluorite (Mohs 4), while cutting perpendicular to the long axis is like cutting quartz (Mohs 7). For Drummond, the real problem with cutting materials like kyanite isn't directional hardness, it is cleavage.

Though kyanite is normally blue, it may also be green, yellow, orange, brown, gray, white or colorless. Blue varieties of kyanite are caused by the presence of iron combined with titanium, much like sapphire. That's why blue kyanite and sapphire are similar in color. Green kyanite, by contrast, owes its color to vanadium. The color of orange kyanite is probably due to manganese, but smaller quantities of chromium, titanium, and vanadium can also be present. Spectra confirm manganese absorption, so Stone Group Labs believes that manganese is the main player in the color of orange kyanite.

Fig. Ky.1 Nepali Kyanite. *Gem and photo: Bear Williams, Stone Group Laboratories.*

Fig. Ky.2 Green kyanite from Brazil. *Gem and photo: Coast-to-Coast Rarestones Intl.*

Fig. Ky.3 Kyanite necklace. *Jewelry and photo by Gurhan.*

Transparent kyanite with a good blue color is found in several places—Brazil, Kenya, India, China, Tanzania, Mozambique, Myanmar, Nepal and the United States (North Carolina). However, since about 2001, Nepal has been the most important source of top-grade blue kyanite, followed by Brazil. Nepali kyanite comes closest to imitating fine sapphire. Recently richly orange colored kyanite has been produced at the same deposit that is worked for orange spessartine in Loliondo, Tanzania.

Industrial grade material occurs more widely in the above-mentioned countries and is also found in Switzerland, Italy, Russia, Australia and various states in the U.S., including Massachusetts, Connecticut, Georgia, Virginia and Vermont. Industrial kyanite is used to produce spark-plugs, electrical insulators, abrasives, porcelain dishware and plumbing fixtures. India is the largest producer of industrial-use kyanite.

Most kyanite in jewelry is fashioned as cabochons or beads, but transparent material is often faceted. Occasionally, kyanite is cut as a cat's-eye cabochon. With the exception of material from Nepal, most transparent kyanite is heavily included. Lower clarity results in lower prices. Commercial quality kyanite is available for less than $50/ct retail. Better quality material in sizes of one-carat and larger retail for roughly $50/ct–$300/ct.

Translucent and fibrous kyanite sells for less than $15/ct and is used to create distinctive jewelry pieces. Semi-opaque non-crystalline material may cost ten dollars or less per stone or it may be sold by the strand as a necklace. Strands of commercial quality kyanite beads are available for less than $100, but expect to pay a few hundred dollars more if the strands are transparent. An intense sapphire blue color is generally the most in demand, but other kyanite colors can also be attractive. Very dark or very light stones generally cost less than more colorful ones in medium to medium-dark tones. Vibrant colors with as little gray as possible command the highest prices.

Fig. Ky.4 Kyanite and moonstone bracelet from Lang Antique and Estate Jewelry. *Photo by Thomas Picarella.*

Fig. Ky.5 Kyanite earrings. *Jewelry created and photographed by Carina Rossner.*

Fig. Ky.6 Kyanite earrings by Yossi Harari. *Photo from Muse Imports.*

Fig. Ky.7 Kyanite and quartz from Brazil. *Specimen from and photo by Claudio Grage.*

Fig. Ky.8 Orange kyanite from Tanzania. *Specimen from and photo by John S. White.*

Larimar (LAR i mar) a variety of pectolite; silicates class, pyroxenoid group
Chemical formula: $NaCa_2Si_3O_8(OH)$, sodium calcium silicate hydroxide

RI: 1.59–1.64, spot 1.60   **Cleavage**: perfect in one direction
Hardness: 4.5–5   **Luster**: vitreous, silky
SG: 2.75–2.90   **Optic char**: DR, biaxial positive; aggregate
Birefringence: .029–.038   **Fracture**: uneven, splintery
Crystal system: triclinic   **Crystal form**: acicular, botryoidal, fibrous, massive
Toughness: fair   **Absorption spectrum**: not diagnostic
Magnetism: inert   **Pleochroism**: none
Fluorescence: inert to moderate greenish yellow to orange (LW & SW; often stronger under SW); may phosphoresce.   **Treatments**: Normally none; the color is natural.
May fade upon prolonged exposure to strong sunlight; fuses easily to heat; dissolves in HCl acid.

"Larimar" is a trade name for a rare Caribbean blue to blue-green gemstone found only in the Dominican Republic, whose color is due to traces of copper in its composition. It is translucent to semi-opaque and is often variegated with white and different shades of blue. The first written record of larimar dates back to 1916; the next record of it is in 1974 when Peace Corps volunteer Norman Rilling and Miguel Méndez, a Dominican native, found the stone. They named it "larimar," which is a combination of "LARIssa" (Méndez's daughter's name) and "MAR" ("sea" in Spanish). Larimar is of volcanic origin and comes from the mountainous, southwestern region of the Dominican Republic, but some small boulders have been washed down the hills, and have been found on the beaches of Barahona, as if larimar came out of the sea. That is how it was found by Rilling and Mendez.

Larimar is mined by hand because dynamite and heavy machinery could destroy it. The mines are often shut down during the five month hurricane season because of torrential rainfall; as a result, larimar sells for more than many other semi-opaque to translucent gems. Nice cabochons are available for less than $100 retail, but they can also cost much more. More often than not, larimar is sold by the piece. The price varies significantly depending on the color, quality, size and weight of a stone. The deeper and more intense blues tend to be more valued than lighter tones, but some people prefer the pastel shades. Translucency, brightness, and clarity also affect the value of larimar, and cracks can lower the price significantly. Patterning is somewhat subjective, but patterns that are interesting and unique with good contrast are generally the most prized.

A high percentage of larimar is sold mounted in jewelry. In addition to the cost of the stone, the metal, workmanship, and skill and prestige of the designer will be factored into the price. Larimar is also sold as carvings and beads. Good quality beads are relatively expensive; 6–7 mm beads usually retail for at least $200/strand; 9–10 mm rounds can retail for $600/strand. Prices can be even higher and have remained so for years.

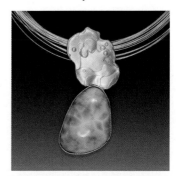

Fig. L.1 Carved larimar slide pendant by Helen Serras-Herman. *Photo: M. J. Colella.*

Fig. L.2 Larimar pendant. *Jewelry and photo by Carina Rossner.*

Magnesite (MAG nuh site), carbonates class, calcite group
Chemical formula: $MgCO_3$, magnesium carbonate not to be confused with magnetite, iron oxide, a gray to black mineral

RI: 1.515–1.717	**Cleavage**: perfect in three directions
Hardness: 3.5–4.5	**Luster**: vitreous to dull
SG: 3.00–3.12	**Optic char**: DR, uniaxial negative, aggregate
Birefringence: .202	**Fracture**: granular to uneven to splintery or conchoidal
Toughness: poor	**Magnetism**: diamagnetic (very weakly repels objects)
Crystal system: hexagonal	**Crystal shape**: fibrous, granular, massive, rhombohedral, prismatic

Fluorescence: blue, green or white glow, SW usually stronger, often greenish phosphorescence
Treatments: frequently dyed and stabilized to imitate other gems and improve durability
Heat may damage dyed magnesite; effervesces only in warm acid unlike calcite which reacts readily with cold acid; massive (non crystalline) magnesite can be very porous, so avoid soaking it in liquids; avoid ultrasonics and steamers.

Named for its magnesium content, magnesite is usually white and semi-opaque, but it may be colorless and transparent or light to dark brown if it has iron impurities. Because of its porosity and ability to accept dyes, semi-opaque massive magnesite is commonly dyed to imitate other stones such as turquoise, lapis lazuli and coral. Magnesite beads and cabochons are inexpensive, with strands retailing for as low as $10 at gem shows and on the Internet. The semi-opaque material is found worldwide including Brazil, Algeria, Australia, Austria, Canada, China, India, Korea, Norway, Sweden and the United States. Transparent magnesite is rare and found in Brazil, primarily in Brumado, Bahia. Faceted stones retail for roughly $30–$60/ct, but are primarily sold to collectors.

Magnesite is easily confused with dolomite, a calcium magnesium carbonate, which is also frequently dyed and has a similar refractive index and hardness. However, magnesite has no response to cold hydrochloric acid, as does dolomite, and is slightly heavier. Magnesite is used more often for beads and cabochons than dolomite.

Besides being used in jewelry and mineral specimens, magnesite is an important industrial mineral. It is a catalyst in the production of synthetic rubber and a binder in flooring material. It is also a good insulating material in the electrical industry because of its high electrical resistance and high thermal conductivity. It is almost impossible to melt magnesite, so it is ideal for furnace linings. In addition, it is used to make magnesium chemicals and pharmaceuticals.

Fig. Mg.1 Brazilian magnesite (17.75 ct). *Courtesy Coast-to-Coast Rarestones International.*

Fig. Mg.2 Dyed magnesite beads. *Photo © Renée Newman.*

Marcasite (MAR ka site), sulfides class, marcasite group
Chemical formula: FeS_2, iron sulfide, easily confused with pyrite, which has the same chemical composition but a different crystal structure.

RI: opaque / not applicable	**Cleavage**: distinct in one direction
Hardness: 6–6.5	**Fracture**: uneven
SG: 4.85–4.92	**Crystal system**: orthorhombic
Toughness: easily chipped	**Crystal shape**: tabular, pyramidal, massive, granular, globular
Luster: metallic	**Magnetism**: nonmagnetic

Treatments: various preservation coatings are used such as vinyl acetate.
Stable to light; surface oxidizes (tarnishes) over time; can deteriorate in normal atmospheric conditions if it is not coated; avoid ultrasonics.

If you are an antique jewelry enthusiast, you are probably familiar with marcasite because it was popular in the Victorian Era and often faceted as rose cuts. It was named in 1845 after an Arabic or Moorish name applied to pyrite and similar metallic bronze colored minerals. Before 1845, "marcasite" meant both pyrite and marcasite. It is difficult to tell the two minerals apart: they both are opaque with a metallic luster and pale brass-yellow color; they have the same chemical composition, Mohs hardness and a similar density. In fact, most stones sold as marcasites are actually pyrite. Both stones are inexpensive and sell at costume-jewelry prices, so from an appraisal standpoint, it doesn't matter whether they are identified as marcasite or pyrite.

There is a difference between the two stones, however. Marcasite is not as suitable for jewelry because it is more brittle and more unstable than pyrite, especially when the humidity is high. Marcasite may react with moisture, producing sulfuric acid as its sulfur component oxidizes, causing it to disintegrate. According to mineralogist John Sinkankas (1915-2002), not all marcasites deteriorate; some mineral dealers set aside all freshly mined specimens for a year and sell only those that show no signs of alteration (*Gemstone & Mineral Data Book*, p. 263). John White, former Curator of Gems & Minerals at the Smithsonian Institution, says "a year is not nearly long enough. At the Smithsonian we had drawers of both pyrite and marcasite from the same localities. Often only some of each would decompose while others would remain stable when there was no apparent difference between them, a great mystery."

Marcasite occurs throughout the world. Notable sources include Mexico, Peru, France, England, China, Russia and the United States. However do not expect to find it in modern jewelry, and even the marcasite jewelry sold in antique stores is likely to be pyrite.

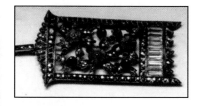  

Figs. Mr.1 & 2 Marcasite jewelry courtesy Skinner (left) and Susanin's (center). *Photos from Gail Brett Levine's www.AuctionMarketResource.com.*

Fig. Mr.3 Marcasite specimen from Folkstone, England. *Courtesy Rob Lavinsky of The Arkenstone.*

Maw-sit-sit: A chromium rich rock composed of kosmochlor, chromite, chrome jadeite, symplectite, chrome-amphibole or amphibole, and a mixture of minor minerals (zeolite, chlorite, albite, serpentine), which fills the spaces between the main mineral components (source: Dr. H. A. Hänni and J. Meyer, 1985)

RI: 1.52–1.74	**Cleavage**: none
Hardness: 6	**Luster**: waxy to vitreous
SG: 2.5–3.2;	**Optic char**: aggregate
Birefringence: none	**Fracture**: granular
Fluorescence: inert	**Pleochroism**: none
Crystal system: monoclinic	**Crystal shape**: massive
Toughness: good	**Absorption spectrum**: not diagnostic

Treatments:: normally not treated except for possible waxing
Stable to light; reaction to chemicals varies with mineral content; ultrasonic risky

Maw-sit-sit is a rare green rock, usually mottled with spots, swirls and veins that are black, various shades of green and sometimes white. The appearance varies depending on the mineral content. First identified in 1963 by Swiss gemologist Eduard J. Gübelin, it was named after the small village of Maw-sit-sit in northwestern Myanmar (Burma) near the area that is still the only source of the material. The location is not far from Burma's famous imperial jadeite mines (Tawmaw), so it is not surprising that before 1963, maw-sit-sit was thought to be a variety of jadeite.

Maw-sit-sit is usually priced by the piece, but sometimes only its carat weight is listed and other times both carat weight and measurements are provided. Stones with an electric emerald green color and nice patterning fetch the highest prices—as much as $50/ct retail, whereas those that are very dark or light-colored and that have large areas of white or black mottling cost the least. For example, a top-grade 10 x 12 mm cabochon might sell for between $100 and $150; prices rise as the size increases. Very low grade stones of the same size can be found for as little as $5. In addition to being sold as cabochons and freeforms, maw-sit-sit is carved and cut as beads. Because of its beauty and rarity, high quality maw-sit-sit is typically set in gold or platinum. A good source of further information is the webpage: http://www.nordskip.com/mawsitsit.html.

Fig. Mw.1 Maw-sit-sit ring by Michael Sugarman. *Photo by Ralph Gabriner.*

Fig. Mw.2 Maw-sit-sit beads and pendant from Dona Dirlam. *Photo © Renée Newman.*

Natural Glass—Obsidian (ob SID ee un), mineraloids class
Moldavite (MOLE duh vite), a variety of tektite and a member of the mineraloids class
Chemical formula: mainly SiO_2, silicon dioxide, also known as silica

RI: 1.48-1.51	**Cleavage**: none
Hardness: 5–5.5	**Luster**: vitreous
SG: 2.33–2.50	**Optic char**: SR, anomalous DR common
Birefringence: none	**Fracture**: conchoidal
Dispersion: none to .010	**Pleochroism**: none
Crystal system: amorphous	**Crystal shape**: massive, round nodules
Toughness: fair to good	**Fluorescence**: generally inert
Spectra: not diagnostic	**Treatments**: normally not treated

Stable to light; melts at low temperatures, avoid thermal shock; attacked by HF acid
Ultrasonic cleaning is usually safe, steamer is risky.

Obsidian is a natural glass formed by the rapid cooling of volcanic lava rich in silica. The lava cooled so fast after flowing into a body of water such as a lake or ocean that it didn't have time to crystallize and become a mineral like quartz. Obsidian is usually black, brown, gray or dark green, but it can also be banded, have a golden or silver sheen, or have snowflake-like patterns. Another variety, called rainbow obsidian, owes its spectral hues to interference of light caused by included layers of tiny bubbles.

Obsidian is found wherever there have been volcanic eruptions with silica-rich lava. Three of the most notable sources are Mexico, Italy and the United States.

Ancient civilizations used obsidian for arrowheads, spearheads, mirrors and cutting tools as well as jewelry. Obsidian is still used today for surgical scalpels because it can be fashioned into blades that are several times sharper than blades of steel. Its primary use, however, is for carvings, spheres, beads and other jewelry. Obsidian is inexpensive and generally priced by the piece. Despite its low prices, man-made glass imitations are sold, particularly on the Internet.

Fig. Ng.1 Obsidian ring. *Created & photographed by Gurhan.*

Fig. Ng.2 Obsidian pendant. *Created & photographed by Carina Rossner.*

Moldavite is a natural glass that may have formed when a meteorite hit the earth. Named after the Moldau River in the Czech Republic where it was discovered in 1787, moldavite is usually olive-green or forest-green and ranges from transparent to semi-opaque.

Tektite is a general term for natural glass that is thought to have been formed from meteorite impact melting the local rock and sand; most are black or brown. Moldavite is the best-known tektite. Because of its rarity and higher transparency, it costs more than obsidian. Transparent faceted stones generally sell for between $20–$50/ct retail, but some exceptionally fine moldavites have retailed for as much as $100/ct. Translucent to semi-opaque stones sell for much less and may be priced by the piece. Green beer bottle glass has been cut to simulate moldavite, so buy it from trusted sources.

Fig. Ng.3 Moldavite (9.39 ct, Czech Republic) with typical flow lines and bubbles, *Gem and photo from Coast-to-Coast Rarestones Intl.*

Fig. Ng.4 Moldavite druse pendant. *Created and photographed by Carina Rossner.*

Fig. Ng.5 Close-up view of rainbow obsidian. *Photo by Carina Rossner.*

Fig. Ng.6 Snowflake obsidian pendant. *Created and photographed by Carina Rossner.*

Fig. Ng.7 Carved obsidian elephant with opal inlay. *Photo by Juan José Virgen Alatorre.*

Fig. Ng.8 Obsidian arrowhead. *Photo by Juan José Virgen Alatorre.*

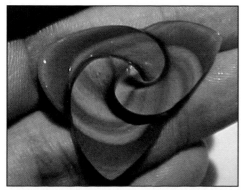

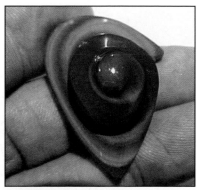

Fig. Ng.9 Banded obsidian. *Photo by Juan José Virgen Alatorre.*

Fig. Ng.10 Banded Obsidian. *Photo by Juan José Virgen Alatorre.*

Phosphosiderite (fos foe SI der ite), phosphates class, metavariscite group
Chemical formula: $Fe^{3+}PO_4 \cdot 2(H_2O)$, hydrated iron phosphate

RI: 1.69–1.74	**Cleavage**: perfect in one direction, distinct in one direction
Hardness: 3.5–4	**Luster**: vitreous to resinous
SG:2.40–2.76	**Optic char**: DR, biaxial negative
Birefringence: .046	**Fracture**: uneven
Crystal system: monoclinic	**Crystal shape**: spherical, crust-like aggregates on matrix
Toughness: brittle	**Trichroism**: pink, red, colorless

Treatments: typically impregnated with a polymer, wax or plastic.
Soluble in hydrochloric acid; avoid ultrasonics and steamers; wash in warm soapy water.

Discovered in 1890, phosphosiderite is named after its chemical composition of phosphorus and iron (*sideros* in Greek). It ranges in color from purple to pink to reddish or colorless. Recently a pink to purple semi-opaque variety appeared on the market and is being used for beads and cabochons. It sometimes has yellow veining of cacoxenite, an iron aluminum phosphate mineral. It is said to be from South America. However, the actual mine source has not been documented yet, so we don't have proof that this new material is natural. It is usually stabilized with a glue, paraffin or epoxy resin before being used in jewelry. Phosphosiderite cabs sell for between about $1 and $80 depending on size and quality. The average retail price for strands of round beads is around $40 to $250.

Fig. Ph.1 Phosphosiderite earrings with yellow veining. *Nevada Mineral & Book Co; photo © Renée Newman.*

Fig. Ph.2 Phosphosiderite beads. *Photo © Renée Newman.*

Fig. Ph.3 Phosphosiderite necklace from Nevada Mineral & Book Co. *Photo ©R. Newman.*

Prehnite (pronounced "PRE nite"), silicates class, phyllosilicates family
Chemical formula: $Ca_2Al_2Si_3O_{10}(OH)_2$, hydrated calcium aluminum silicate

RI: 1.616-1.649 (spot 1.63)	**Cleavage**: good in one direction
Hardness: 6–6.5	**Luster**: vitreous, waxy
SG: 2.8–2.95	**Optic char**: DR, biaxial positive, usually aggregate reaction
Birefringence: .020–.033	**Fracture**: uneven, conchoidal
Dispersion: none	**Crystal system**: orthorhombic
Pleochroism: none	**Crystal shape**: globular, stalactitic, botryoidal masses
Toughness: fair to good	**Fluorescence**: inert to dull brownish yellow
Spectrum: weak line at 438 nm	**Magnetism**: green – weak to moderate

Treatments: occasionally impregnated with wax or polymers, fracture filling is possible. Sensitive to heat; attacked by acids; avoid ultrasonics and steam cleaners.

Most prehnite is translucent and green to yellowish green, but it may also be semi-transparent to transparent (very rare) and yellow, orange, brown, gray, white, colorless or in rare cases pink. Some fibrous material is cut to show a cat's-eye effect. First discovered in South Africa by Dutch mineralogist Colonel Henrik Von Prehn (1733-1785), prehnite was the first mineral known to be named after a person.

The majority of the world's prehnite comes from Australia, but it is also found in Mali, Tanzania, China, India, South Africa, Germany, France, Scotland, New Zealand, Switzerland, Quebec, Canada and the USA.

Prehnite may be faceted but it is usually carved or cut as cabochons or beads. It is also used for book-ends, clock faces, desk sets and inlay. When cut, prehnite may be confused with jade, serpentine, smithsonite, chrysoprase, peridot or green beryl. It is relatively inexpensive and typically ranges from around $5/ct–$50/ct. Even though prehnite is available in sizes above five carats, it is difficult to find large stones free from inclusions. High quality clean semitransparent stones can retail for as much as $100/ct in large sizes.

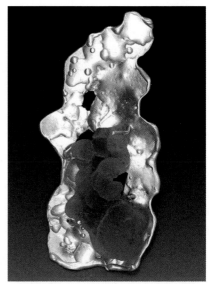

Fig. Pr.1 Prehnite and enamel pendant by Hubert Inc. *Photo by Josian Gattermeier.*

Fig. Pr.2 Prehnite pendant. *Created and photographed by Carina Rossner.*

Fig. Pr.3 "Fingers" of prehnite from Prospect Park Quarry, New Jersey. *Specimen and photo from Rob Lavinsky of The Arkenstone.*

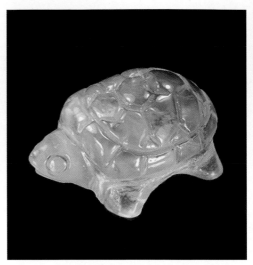

Fig. Pr.4 Mali prehnite carving. *Prehnite turtle and photo from Rob Lavinsky of The Arkenstone.*

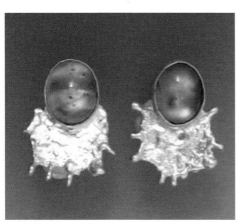

Fig. Pr.5 Prehnite earrings. *Crafted and photographed by Carina Rossner.*

Fig. Pr.6 Rare pink prehnite (manganoan) with grossular (Jeffrey Mine, Asbestos, Quebec, Canada). *Rob Lavinsky of The Arkenstone.*

Fig. Pr.7 Prehnite and diamond bracelet by Assil auctioned by Sotheby's NY 9-25-2008; hammer price: $9,375.00. *Sotheby's photo from Gail Levine of www.AuctionMarketResource.com.*

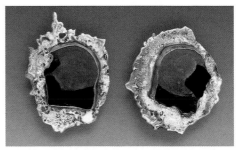

Fig. Pr.8 Prehnite and epidote earrings. *Crafted and photographed by Carina Rossner.*

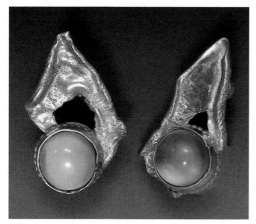

Fig. Pr.9 Prehnite earrings. *Crafted & photographed by Carina Rossner.*

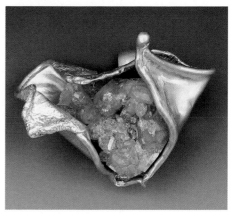

Fig. Pr.10 Prehnite pendant. *Crafted & photographed by Carina Rossner.*

Fig. Pr. 11 Tumbled Tanzanian prehnite. *Stones and photo courtesy of New Era Gems.*

Fig. Pr.12 Faceted Australian prehnite. *Courtesy Coast-to-Coast Rarestones Intl.*

Fig. Pr.13 Prehnite bead necklace by Amy Kahn Russell. *Photo © Renée Newman.*

Psilomelane (sil LAHM uh lane), a mixture of black manganese oxide minerals of which romanèchite is a major component. Formerly, it was a group and mineral species name. Romanèchite chemical formula: $(BaH_2O)_2Mn_5O_{10}$, barium and manganese hydrous oxide

Hardness: 5–6	**Luster**: sub metallic, dull
SG: 4.4–4.72	**Magnetism**: nonmagnetic
Cleavage: none	**Fracture**: uneven
Crystal system: monoclinic	**Crystal shape**: botryoidal aggregate, massive, kidney-shaped
Toughness: good	**Fluorescence**: inert

Treatments: Normally none except for possible fracture filling. It is possible to coat drusy psilomelane with titanium.
Stable to light; soluble in hydrochloric acid; wash with warm soapy water.

Psilomelane is a black opaque rock which offers designers distinctive designs, surfaces, and textures. Some polished stones have interesting patterns created by their varied composition. Others have a botryoidal surface, which resembles a cluster of grapes. Some psilomelane cabochons have a surface crust covered by tiny black sparkling crystals, which is called **druse**. Unlike black onyx or black quartz druse, which is dyed, psilomelane has a natural jet black color. Most of the psilomelane used in jewelry is intimately ingrown with quartz, which gives it sufficient toughness to take a fine polish and resist wear.

The name "psilomelane" originates from the Greek *psilos* - "smooth" and *melas* - "black" in reference to the stone's appearance. Psilomelane has been used as a substitute for hematite in jewelry; as a result, it is sometimes erroneously called black hematite.

The Silver Crown Mine in Chihuahua, Mexico is noted for its psilomelane mixed with cryptocrystalline quartz, and it has a Mohs hardness rating ranging from 5–7. Since it is black with silver banding and swirls, it is sometimes incorrectly referred to as black malachite. The mine is closed due to cave-in problems, but rough from there is still being sold.

Sources of psilomelane besides Mexico include England, Germany, Brazil, Nova Scotia, Canada, and the US states of Virginia, Vermont, Michigan, Arkansas and New Mexico. Normally priced by the piece, psilomelane cabochons typically retail for around $5–$200 depending on the size and attractiveness of the stone.

Fig. Ps.1 Drusy psilomelane. *Pendant by Tom DeGasperis; photo: Shelly Smith.*

Fig. Ps.2 Drusy psilomelane pin design © by Eve J. Alfillé. *Photo by Matthew Arden.*

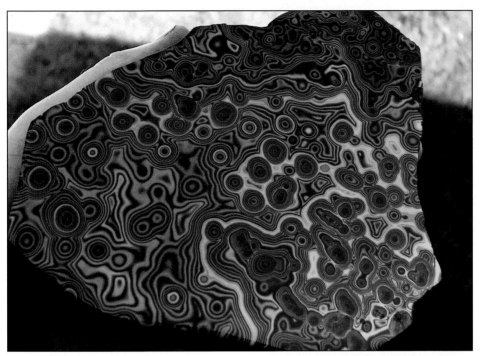

Fig. Ps.3 Psilomelane (Chihuahua, Mexico) & photo: Philip Stephenson of RareRocksAndGems.

Fig. Ps.5 Plume formation psilomelane. *Photo by Jeff and Lynn Hill.*

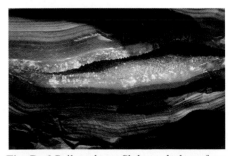

Fig. Ps.4 Psilomelane inlay pendant by Mark Anderson of Different Seasons Jewelry. *Photo by Jessica Dow.*

Fig. Ps.6 Psilomelane. *Slabs and photo from Mark Anderson of Different Seasons Jewelry.*

Pyrite (PIE rite), sulfides class, pyrite group
Chemical formula: FeS_2, iron sulfide, easily confused with marcasite, which has the same chemical composition but a different crystal structure.

RI: opaque / not applicable	**Cleavage**: indistinct in one direction
Hardness: 6–6.5	**Fracture**: conchoidal, uneven
SG: 4.85–5.10	**Luster**: metallic
Toughness: easily chipped	**Magnetism**: nonmagnetic, but magnetic after heating
Crystal system: cubic	**Crystal shape**: cubes, octahedra, pyritohedra, druse, nodules, discs
Fluorescence: inert	**Absorption spectrum**: not diagnostic

Treatments: Much pyrite used in jewelry is coated with polymer resins to help prevent it from oxidizing and breaking down to a black powder that will rub off on clothing; some pyrite is coated with substances such as silver molybdenite and gold to give it a different color. Reconstituted hematite is difficult to distinguish from natural hematite and may require lab testing. Stable to light; fuses under jeweler's torch; soluble in nitric acid; surface oxidizes (tarnishes) over time; can deteriorate in normal atmospheric conditions if it is not coated.

Sometimes called "fool's gold," pyrite is a shiny, brassy yellow mineral. Even though it resembles gold, it is easy to distinguish the two; gold is much heavier (SG of 19.3 versus 5), but pyrite is harder and cannot be scratched with a fingernail or pocket knife. It was named from the Greek *pyro* for "fire" because sparks flew from it when hit with another mineral or metal.

Pyrite has been used in jewelry for centuries. Native American Indians also used it as mirrors. Even though pyrite is a common mineral seldom sold in the average jewelry store, it is included in this book because it is an unusual stone. Nevertheless, it is becoming more popular, especially for men's jewelry, which sometimes features pyrite crystals on slate. Designers like to use pyrite crystals and druse in jewelry because of their unique textures and shapes. Iridescent pyrite and rainbow pyrite druse have natural iridescence, but some pyrite is colored by an artificial coating. Pyrite is also cut as beads, carvings, spheres, cabochons or faceted stones, often rose cuts; specimens are popular among mineral collectors. Fossils are sometimes replaced by pyrite. When cleaned and polished, they can be used for bola ties, key chains and other objects.

Most pyrite jewelry is inexpensive; a strand of tumbled beads, for example, may retail for as little as $10, but beads with distinctive crystal shapes or that are nuggets will cost more. Because of its high density, a pyrite necklace will feel heavy. As for rainbow pyrite druse, the color and the degree of brightness and even crystal formation of the druse determine its value; red iridescence is the most desired. Carvings and designer pieces are priced by the piece and cost significantly more than mass-produced jewelry because you are also paying for the workmanship and creativity of the designer.

Fig. Py.1 Drusy rainbow pyrite necklace (26.18 ct) by Helen Serras-Herman. *Photo by* M. J. Colella.

Pyrite is found worldwide, but Peru, Spain, Mexico, Brazil and the United States are particularly noted for their distinctive pyrite specimens. Drusy rainbow pyrite is found near the Volga River, at Ulyanovsk, in Russia.

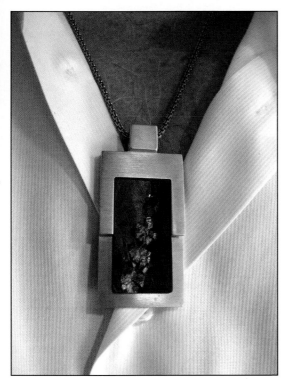

Fig. Py.3 Pyrite-on-slate pendant worn by the designer Frédéric Duclos. *Photo © Renée Newman.*

Fig. Py.3 Pyrite dinosaur gembone pendant by Mark Anderson of Different Seasons Jewelry. *Photo by Jessica Dow.*

Fig. Py.4 Striated pyrite crystals from the Quiruvilca District, La Libertad Department, Peru. *Specimen from Pala International; photo by John McLean.*

Fig. Py.5 Pyrite in marl from Navajun, Logroño Province, Spain. *Specimen from and photo by John S. White.*

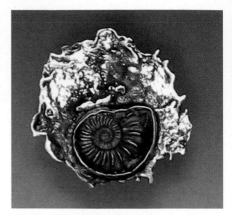

Fig. Py.6 Pyrite-in-jasper pendant by Fred and Kate Pearce of Pearce Design. *Photo by Ralph Gabriner.*

Fig. Py.7 Pyratized ammonite earring. *Jewelry and photo by Carina Rossner.*

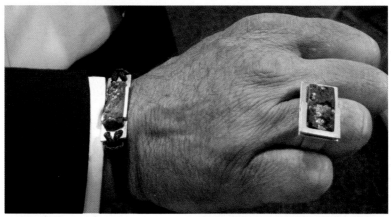

Fig. Py.8 Pyrite-on-slate bracelet and ring worn by the designer Frédéric Duclos. *Photo © Renée Newman.*

Fig. Py.9 Pyrite burst pendant. *Jewelry & photo: Jamie Joseph Designs, Inc.*

Fig. Py.10 Iridescent pyrite on calcite from Santa Eulalia, Chihuahua, Mexico. *Specimen and photo from Rob Lavinsky of The Arkenstone.*

Rhodochrosite (row dow CROW site), carbonates class, calcite group
Chemical formula: $MnCO_3$, manganese carbonate

RI: 1.578–1.840   **Cleavage**: perfect in three directions, but usually obscured
Hardness: 3.5–4.5   **Luster**: vitreous, pearly
SG: 3.4–3.7 pure: 3.7   **Optic char**: DR, uniaxial negative, aggregate
Birefringence: .201–.220   **Fracture**: uneven to granular
Dispersion: .015   **Toughness**: fair
Crystal system: trigonal   **Crystal shape**: rhombohedrons, curved masses, rosettes
Magnetism: picks up   **Treatments**: occasionally heat-treated, fracture filling is possible
Pleochroism: moderate to strong orangy yellow and red or orange-pink; none in aggregate
Absorption spectrum: Bands at 551nm and 410nm, and weak lines at around 450 and 545nm
Fluorescence: none to moderate pink (LW), none to weak red (SW)
Stable to light; turns brown, gray or black and breaks into pieces under a jeweler's torch;
effervesces in warm hydrochloric acid; avoid acids, ultrasonics and steam cleaners.

Rhodochrosite, whose name means "rose coloring" in Greek, can have either a solid pink to red to orange color, or may be variegated and banded with different shades of pink resembling agate banding. The banded material is translucent to semi-opaque, and most of it is found in Argentina. Much of the material is carved into ornamental figurines or cut as spheres; some of it is used for cabochons or beads, and stalactitic rhodochrosite is sliced into attractive bull's eye patterned discs. Rhodochrosite beads are moderately priced, but the selection may be limited. Plan on paying at least $100 for a nice 15-16 inch strand of round 5mm+ beads. As the bead size increases, the price rises. Cabochons vary widely in price. The pattern, thickness, translucency, clarity, color and size affect their value.

Fig. Rc.1 Banded rhodochrosite. *Necklace and photo from Kothari.*

In 1974, South Africa became an important source of translucent to transparent solid-color rhodochrosite when it was discovered in the N'Chwaning mine in the Kalahari desert region of Cape Province. Production in South Africa is very limited now, however.

Fig. Rc.2 Rhodochrosite from Hotazel, South Afica. *Coast-to-Coast Rare Gemstones Intl.*

Fig. Rc.3 Rhodochrosite (N'Chwaning Mine, South Africa). *The Arkenstone.*

The Sweet Home mine in Alma, Colorado has produced much of the world's finest rhodochrosite. Intense red crystals have been known in Colorado since the 1880's, but it wasn't until the early 1990's that mining techniques were developed to recover them economically. Unfortunately, the mine ceased operation in 2004 and prices of fine red Colorado stones have increased dramatically since then. Expect to pay more than $1000/ct for fine-quality Sweet Home gems above five carats, if you can find them.

Fig. Rc.4 Rhodochrosite (Sweet Home Mine, Colorado). *Coast-to-Coast Rare Gemstones*

Fig. Rc.5 Rhodochrosite (Sweet Home Mine). *The Arkenstone; photo by Joe Budd.*

Peru has also produced pink to red gem quality crystals that compete with those of Colorado and South Africa. Brazil and Quebec, Canada are other sources of rhodochrosite. Recently, a fair amount of rhodochrosite has come out of China. The material has an orangy pink color similar to padparadscha and was introduced at the 2009 Tucson gem show. According to Paul Cory of Iteco Inc, many of the stones being sold now as Sweet Home Mine rhodochrosites are actually from China." He adds, "It looks like the China mine will be shutting down soon, or at least redirect efforts toward metal mining, so I would expect to see the prices [of rhodochrosite] rise."

Retail prices for one- to three-carat faceted rhodochrosites are around $200/ct– $800/ct, but fine stones of three carats are very rare. Larger sizes may sell for more, and translucent cabochons sell for much less. Most faceted rhodochrosite has eye visible inclusions and is semitransparent to translucent, so clarity and transparency are key price factors along with carat weight. For additional photos and information on rhodochrosite, consult Renée Newman's *Exotic Gems, Volume 1.*

Fig. Rc.6 Rhodochrosite ring by Susan Sadler. *Photo by Jeffrey Mobley*

Fig. Rc.7 Rhodochrosite ring by Mary Esses. *Photo courtesy of Mary Esses.*

Fig. Rc.8 Rhodochrosite earrings. *Jewelry and photo by Gurhan.*

Fig. Rc.9 Argentinian rhodochrosite beads and cabochon from Paul Cory of Iteco, Inc. *Photo by Jeff Scovil.*

Fig. Rc.10 Rhodochrosite earrings. *Made and photographed by Carina Rossner.*

Fig. Rc. 11 Rhodochrosite pendant. *Made and photographed by Carina Rossner.*

Fig. Rc.12 Rhodochrosite beads and pendant from Stonesmith Jewelers. *Photo © Renée Newman.*

Rhodonite (ROW dow NITE), silicates class, pyroxene group
Chem. formula: $MnSiO_3$, manganese silicate, (not to be confused with rhodolite, a garnet)

RI: 1.72–1.75 spot: ≈1.73   **Cleavage**: perfect in 2 directions, distinct in 1 (none in massive)
Hardness: 5.5–6.5   **Luster**: vitreous, subvitreous, dull
SG: 3.50–3.76 pure: 3.67   **Optic char**: DR, biaxial positive, aggregate
Birefringence: .010–.014   **Fracture**: uneven, granular
Crystal system: triclinic   **Crystal shape**: tabular, massive, granular
Magnetism: picks up   **Fluorescence**: none to medium or deep red (LW)
Toughness: good in aggregates to poor in transparent stones, especially those with cleavages
Pleochroism: weak to moderate orange-red and brownish-red; none in aggregate material
Absorption spectrum: broad bands centered around 545nm and a line at 503 nm
Treatments: sometimes impregnated and/or dyed, fracture filling is possible
Stable to light; fuses easily into a brownish or black glass under a jeweler's torch; attacked slightly by acids; ultrasonics are risky.

Rhodonite and rhodochrosite are similar in many ways: they both have a gorgeous rose pink color range which extends to orange-red; they both can be transparent to semi-opaque; they both may have a solid color or be variegated with black veining, although black markings are much more common in rhodonite and the patterns are different. In addition, rhodonite normally does not have the distinctive agate-like banding found in Argentinian rhodonite. However, when rhodonite and rhodochrosite have the same uniform color, it is difficult to tell them apart by sight alone. Rhodonite has

Fig. Rn.2 Rhodonite box with Russian hallmarks auctioned 12-14-2000 by Christie's East. Hammer price: $3,878. *Photo from Gail Levine of www.AuctionMarketResource.com.*

the advantage of being harder and therefore more resistant to scratching. Because of the perfect cleavage of transparent rhodonite and rhodochrosite, they both are susceptible to chipping and are poor choices for everyday rings. In aggregate form, they are more durable and better suited for rings. According to master cutter John Bradshaw, cutting rhodonite is significantly more difficult than cutting rhodochrosite.

Fig. Rn.2 Rhodonite (Lafayette Mine, Brazil). *Coast-to-Coast Rare Gemstones International.*

Fig. Rn.3 Rhodonite (1.08 ct) from Brazil. *Coast-to-Coast Rare Gemstones International.*

Thanks to recent finds in Brazil as a byproduct of manganese mining, transparent to semi-transparent rhodonite is more available now than it was in the 1900's. However, much of it is heavily included. Transparent facetable rhodonite has also come from Broken Hill, NSW, Australia, but it is exceedingly rare. The pricing is similar to that of rhodochrosite, with faceted rhodonites retailing from around 200/ct–800/ct. Exceptional stones can cost more, whereas translucent cabochons may be less than $100/ct. If translucent solid-color cabochons have been impregnated with a wax or polymer, they generally sell for less than untreated rhodonites, sometimes about half the price of untreated material.

Most of the rhodonite on the market is an aggregate—a rock, typically with black inclusions and veining. Sources include Russia, Australia, Brazil, Peru, Madagascar, South Africa, Sweden, India, and the United States This material is carved into decorative objects and cut as beads and cabochons. It is normally priced by the piece. Nice cabochons are available for less than $100.

Fig. Rn.4 Rhodonite pin/pendant by Amy Kahn Russell. *Photo by Noelle Feucht.*

Fig. Rn.5 Rhodonite from Martin Mine, Huanuco, Peru. *Specimen & photo from Rob Lavinsky of The Arkenstone.*

Astorite: A trade name for a predominantly pink rock of varying tints that is composed of rhodonite, rhodochrosite, chalcedony and sometimes silver and flecks of gold or pyrite, which is from the Toltec mine in the San Juan Mountains of Southwestern Colorado. Because of its mixed composition, astorite is typically variegated with black and white spots and veining. Named for John Jacob Astor, a previous owner of the mine, it is used for carvings and cut into cabochons of various size and shapes for jewelry. Mass-produced cabs often sell for less than $30 per piece. Prices of custom-carved astorite pieces depend on the skill and reputation of the carver as well as the attractiveness of the material.

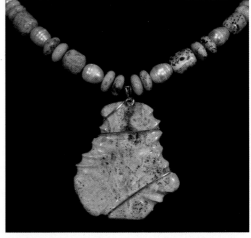

Fig. Rn.3 Carved astorite wire-wrap pendant by gem sculptor Helen Serras-Herman on a strand of astorite beads. *Photo by M. J. Colella.*

Serpentine, a group of minerals in the silicates class
Chemical formula: $(Mg,Fe,Ni)_3Si_2O_5(OH)_4$, magnesium silicate hydroxide

RI: 1.553–1.574   **Cleavage**: perfect 1 direction but not relevant for massive material
Hardness: 2.5–6   **Luster**: waxy, pearly, greasy, vitreous
SG: 2.35–2.65   **Optic char**: (DR) aggregate
Dispersion: none   **Birefringence**: usually not detectable;
Crystal system: monoclinic   **Crystal shape**: usually massive, sometimes fibrous, crystals rare
Toughness: fair   **Fracture**: granular, uneven
Pleochroism: none   **Fluorescence**: inert to weak green (LW)
Magnetism: drags to picks up **Treatments**: dyeing and impregnation with wax or polymers
Stable to light; fuses with difficulty under jeweler's torch; decomposed by hydrochloric and
sulfuric acids; avoid heat, solvents and ultrasonics.

Serpentine is a mineral group that is typically light to dark yellowish green, although it may also be yellow, green, bluish green, gray, brown or black. Its name comes from the word "serpent" because it often resembles the skin of a snake. Most serpentine is translucent to semi-opaque, but it may also be semitransparent and faceted. The two main types of serpentine used in jewelry are bowenite, the state gem of Rhode Island and the hardest stone in the group, and williamsite, which often has black chromite inclusions. Bowenite carvings and jewelry from China are often sold as "new jade" or "jade" because of their close resemblance.

Fig. S.1 Afghanistan bowenite (serpentine). *The Arkenstone.*

Some serpentine displays a cat's-eye effect and a few rare stones appear purplish in incandescent light (see photos below). Such stones have been sold as alexandrite.

Figs S.2 & 3 Left: A dark bluish green serpentine in daylight. Right: same stone appears purple in fiberoptic light. *Photos by Gagan Choudhary, Gem Testing Laboratory, Jaipur, India.*

According to the *GIA Gem Reference Guide*, serpentine is commonly impregnated with wax to improve its appearance by hiding pores and surface cracks. As a result, it is best to avoid heat and solvents.

Though not often seen in jewelry stores, serpentine is a very common mineral, and may also be a component of marble and other rocks. The most important sources of serpentine are China, Russia, Afghanistan, India, Pakistan, South Africa, and the United States, but it is also found elsewhere throughout the world.

Most serpentine is low priced with cabochons typically selling for less than $30. Strands can retail from around $5–$200 depending on size and quality. Expect to pay much more for semi-transparent material and serpentine used in designer jewelry. Faceted semi-transparent serpentine can cost as much as $200/ct. Much serpentine is used for carvings and is often misrepresented as nephrite jade. It is also used as a building stone and for kitchen counter and bar tops.

Fig. S.4 Serpentine pendant. *Created & photographed by Carina Rossner.*

Fig. S.5 Serpentine pendant. *Created and photographed by Carina Rossner.*

Fig. S.6 Maryland williamsite. *Carving courtesy of and photographed by John White.*

Below: Fig. S.8 Arts & Crafts Era serpentine necklace auctioned by Skinner 3/15/2011 for $4,622.00. *Skinner photo from Gail Levine of www. AuctionMarketResource.com*

Fig. S.7 Cat's-eye serpentine. *Gagan Choudhary, Gem Testing Laboratory, Jaipur, India.*

Seraphinite (ser AF i nite), a variety of **clinochlore**; silicates class, chlorite group
Chemical formula: $H_8Mg_5Al_2Si_3O_{18}$, magnesium, aluminum, silicate hydroxide

RI: 1.571–1.599　　　　　**Cleavage**: perfect in one direction
Hardness: 2–2.5　　　　　**Luster**: greasy, pearly, dull
SG: 2.55–2.75　　　　　　**Optic char**: DR, biaxial positive, aggregate
Birefringence: .005–.011　**Fracture**: granular, uneven, splintery, conchoidal
Crystal system: monoclinic　**Crystal shape**: massive, fibrous, tabular, granular
Fluorescence: inert　　　　**Pleochroism**: visible
Treatments: can be impregnated with wax, polymers or plastic to improve polish and durability

　　Seraphinite is a trade name for a distinctive forest green clinochlore variegated with silvery chatoyant fibers. The name was derived from the Hebrew word *seraph* (a celestial being with three pairs of wings) in reference to its feathery wing patterns.

　　Seraphinite comes from the Korshunovskaia Mine near Baikal Lake in Eastern Siberia Russia. The mineral clinochlore was found and described by Russian mineralogist Niolai Kokasharov (1818–1892). Round seraphinite beads retail for roughly $30–$200 per strand; large attractive cabochons are available for less than $100 retail. Spheres, carvings, pendants, earrings, bracelets and necklaces are sold by the piece. Seraphinite is an easy stone to identify with the unaided eye because no other stone looks like it.

Fig. Se.1 Seraphinite. *Slice and photo from John S. White.*

Fig. Se.2 Seraphinite pendant. *Created and photographed by Carina Rossner.*

Fig. Se.3 Seraphinite jewelry from Stonesmith Jewelry. *Photo © Renée Newman.*

Sodalite (SO da lite) silicates class, cancrinite-sodalite group
Hackmanite (HACK ma nite) a pink or lavender variety of sodalite that can fade to colorless or white
Chemical formula: $Na_8Al_6Si_6O_{24}Cl_2$, complex sodium aluminum silicate chloride

RI: 1.480–1.487	**Cleavage**: poor in one direction
Hardness: 5.5–6	**Luster**: vitreous, greasy
SG: 2.15–2.30	**Optic char**: SR or aggregate
Birefringence: none	**Fracture**: subconchoidal, uneven
Dispersion: .018	**Crystal system**: cubic
Toughness: fair to good	**Crystal form**: dodecahedral, octahedral, massive
Magnetism: weak	**Pleochroism**: none

Luminescence: might fluoresce patchy orange or red to LW and SW; yellowish phosphorescence; hackmanite is tenebrescent, lavender or pink fading to white or colorless
Absorption spectrum: usually not diagnostic
Treatments: sometimes fracture filled with oil or Opticon; occasionally dyed
Stability to light: pink fades, but otherwise stable; fuses to a colorless glass; heat can destroy tenebrescence; attacked by HCl; avoid ultrasonics; clean with warm soapy water.

Named in 1811 for its sodium content, sodalite is usually dark blue to violet-blue with white and sometimes yellow or red veining. It is typically semi-opaque to translucent but can also be transparent and colorless or light blue, thanks to discoveries of new deposits. Much sodalite resembles lapis lazuli; in fact sodalite is a component of lapis lazuli, but sodalite rarely contains pyrite inclusions. In addition, sodalite is more translucent than lapis lazuli and has a lower density.

Fig. So.1 Tajikistan sodalite. *Pala International/Mia Dixon.*

Ontario and British Columbia in Canada have produced a significant amount of sodalite; in fact it has even erroneously been referred to as "Canadian lapis." Other sources include Russia, India, Germany, Italy, Norway, Bolivia and the north-eastern United States. Transparent sodalite has been found at Mont St. Hilaire, Quebec, Canada and in Tajikistan. Semi-opaque veined sodalite sells at costume jewelry prices and is used for beads and cabochons. It is also polished into slabs for inlays in objects such as clock cases, boxes and cameos. Faceted transparent blue sodalite is so rare that there is no established pricing system, but a one-carat stone could retail from $100/ct–$1000/ct or more.

Fig. So.2 Sodalite earrings by Amy Kahn Russell. *Photo by Noelle Fuecht.*

Fig. So.3 Cameo with sodalite and other gems. *Pin and photo from Lang Antiques & Estate Jewelry.*

Hackmanite is a pink or purple variety of sodalite that is transparent to translucent and often has a unique property called **tenebrescence**; it either fades to colorless when exposed to light or it becomes darker after exposure to SW UV lighting. For example, when exposed to SW UV, Afghan hackmanite can darken to light to medium violet over a period of 3-5 minutes. Burmese hackmanite, however, can darken to intense dark violet in a matter of seconds. Sunlight has no effect on most Afghan hackmanite. Burmese hackmanite, however, will gradually darken over a period of 1-5 minutes when exposed to sunlight. (From: www.gemologyproject.com/wiki/index.php?title=Hackmanite.)

Besides being tenebrescent, hackmanite fluoresces orange under long-wave ultraviolet light and light orange under short-wave ultraviolet light.

Fig. So.4 Lavender hackmanite from Afghanistan (7.87 ct). *Pala International / Mia Dixon.*

Fig. So.5 Same hackmanite viewed under long-wave ultraviolet light. *Pala International / Mia Dixon.*

The webpage, http://www.gemologyonline.com/hackmanite.html, reports that pink hackmanite from Greenland fades to colorless when exposed to light, but that it returns to its original pink color when placed in the dark for an extended period of time or when exposed to SW UV light. Heating the stone will destroy the tenebrescence. Mont St.Hilaire, Quebec and Tajikistan are two additional sources of tenebrescent hackmanite.

Translucent hackmanite generally retails for around $20/ct–$150/ct whereas transparent hackmanite typically retails from about $150/ct–$1800/ct. Stones with pronounced tenebrescence, high transparency, good clarity and a high-quality cut cost the most.

Fig. So.6 Colorless sodalite from Afghanistan (3.24 ct). *Coast-to-Coast Rarestones Intl.*

Fig. So.7 Burmese hackmanite from Pala International. *Photo: Wimon Manorotkul.*

Sphene (SFEEN), silicates class; also called **titanite**, a name preferred by the International Mineral Association. Gemologists, however, call gem-quality titanite "sphene." Chemical formula: $CaTiSiO_5$, calcium titanium silicate

RI: 1.88–2.05	**Cleavage**: distinct in two directions
Hardness: 5–5.5	**Luster**: adamantine to subadamantine
SG: 3.4–3.6	**Optic char:** DR, biaxial positive
Birefringence: .100–.135	**Fracture**: conchoidal to splintery
Dispersion: .051	**Fluorescence**: usually inert
Crystal system: monoclinic	**Crystal shape**: wedge-shaped & often twinned, prismatic, massive
Toughness: fair	**Absorption spectrum**: sometimes 580 nm doublet

Trichroism: yellow to brown stones—moderate to strong light yellow, brownish orange and brownish yellow; green stones: greenish yellow, reddish yellow and nearly colorless
Treatments: Brown material may be heat-treated to produce orange or reddish brown colors. Stable to light; very sensitive to changes in heat; attacked by acids; ultrasonic cleaning is risky.

If you'd like a green or yellow stone that's as brilliant as a diamond and has more fire, then sphene is the right gem for you. Sphene is noted for its high dispersion (fire, sparkles of rainbow colors). If the stone is colored by chromium, it can have an almost emerald-like green color; chrome-green sphenes fetch the highest prices. In addition to its usual colors of green, yellowish green and yellow, sphene may also be brown or orange. The only disadvantage with sphene is that it can chip easily, so it is best to limit its use in rings for dressy occasions instead of everyday wear. Sphene is ideal for pendants, earrings and brooches.

Sphene is named after the Greek word for a wedge because of its wedge-shaped crystals. Its mineralogical name, "titanite," refers to its titanium content. Thanks to increased availability, sphene is becoming better known. Madagascar has been

Fig. Sp.2 Sphene with good dispersion. *Ring & photo courtesy Richard Krementz Gemstones.*

the largest producer, but sphene is also found in Brazil, Mexico, India, Pakistan, Sri Lanka, Myanmar, Switzerland, Austria, Afghanistan, Russia, Namibia, Canada and the USA.

Considering its beauty and uniqueness, sphene is a good value for the money. Stones below two carats generally retail for about $15/ct–$200/ct; those above two carats can reach $600/ct retail. It's a challenge to find sphenes without eye-visible inclusions in larger sizes. Consequently, clarity has a significant impact on price, particularly if the stones have good dispersion, an intense green color, and a designer-quality cut.

Fig. Sp.1 Tanzanian chrome sphene cut by J. L. White Fine Gemstones. *Photo by Jeff White.*

Fig. Sp.3 A rare color-change sphene (1.78 ct) viewed in daylight (left) and incandescent light (right) from Mayer & Watt. *Photos by Geoffrey Watt.*

Fig. Sp.4 Twinned sphene crystal from Namibia. *Specimen and photo from Rob Lavinsky of The Arkenstone.*

Fig. Sp.5 Sphene cut by John Dyer. *Photo by Lydia Dyer.*

Fig. Sp.6 Sphene cut by Clay Zava, *Pendant and photo courtesy of Cynthia Renée, Inc.*

Fig. Sp.7 Burmese sphene (40.33 ct) from Pala International. *Photo: Jason Stephenson.*

Fig. Sp.8 Sphene rough from Badakshan, Afghanistan courtesy J. L. White Fine Gemstones. *Photo by Jeff White.*

Fig. Sp.9 The sphene cut from rough in previous photo. *Cut and photographed by Jeff White.*

Fig. Sp.10 Sphene from Sri Lanka. *Cut and photographed by Coast-to-Coast Rarestones.*

Fig. Sp.11 Madagascar sphene from J. L. White Fine Gemstones. *Photo by Jeff White.*

Fig. Sp.12 Sphene from Pakistan. *Gem and photo courtesy Columbia Gems House, Inc.*

Fig. Sp.13 Sphene ring. *Jewelry and photo courtesy Timeless Gems and Andrew Sarosi.*

Sugilite (SU jih lite), silicates class, osumilite group
Chemical formula: $(K, Na)(Na, Fe)_2(Li_2Fe)Si_{12}O_{30}$, sodium potassium lithium silicate hydrate, a complex silicate colored by manganese and often mixed with chalcedony (quartz)

Hardness: 5.5–6.5	**RI**: 1.602–1.611, might also be about 1.54 from quartz impurities
Luster: waxy, vitreous	**Cleavage**: poor in one direction
SG: 2.69–2.79	**Optic char**: DR, uniaxial negative, aggregate
Birefringence: none to .003	**Fracture**: granular, sub-conchoidal
Fluorescence: inert	**Magnetism**: drags to picks up
Crystal system: trigonal	**Crystal shape**: massive, granular, prismatic,
Toughness: good	**Spectra**: band at 550 nm; lines at 411, 419, 437, and 445 nm
Pleochroism: none	**Treatments**: sometimes dyed or stabilized with wax or polymers

Stable to light and heat; attacked by HF acid; ultrasonics are risky; warm soapy water is safe.

Most sugilite used in jewelry has a striking purple to magenta color and ranges from translucent to semi-opaque. It can also be yellow-brown, violet, pink, or black. Sugilite was named for petrologist Ken-ichi Sugi, who discovered the mineral in Japan in 1944. However, the first commercial sugilite deposit was not found until 1979 in the Wessels mine near Hotazel, South Africa during mining operations for manganese ore. Sugilite has also been reported in India, Canada and Italy.

According to GIA research documented in the summer 1987 issue of *Gems & Gemology* (pp. 78–89), there are two types of gem materials called sugilite. One is predominantly **manganoan sugilite** (manganese-bearing sugilite) with minor mineral impurities, and the other is chalcedony mixed with (and colored by) sugilite. The textural appearance and coloration of both sugilite and stones intermixed with chalcedony can range from uniform to mottled, veined or layered, depending on the homogeneity of the material. When observed with a microscope, all of the GIA samples (even those with a uniform color) were found to consist of interlocking grains of sugilite and other minerals.

Fig. Su.1 Sugilite inlay ring by Randy Polk Designs. *Photo from Randy Polk.*

The GIA research team found that sugilite can fracture along irregular surfaces, but the material used for jewelry is generally quite tough and durable. Cleavage was not evident in their samples, which varied from opaque to translucent.

No apparent relationship existed between the degree of transparency and the sugilite and chalcedony content. It was during RI (refractive index) testing that the GIA noted the two types of sugilite mentioned above. Sixteen of the 25 samples gave a non-varying reading of 1.607 as expected for sugilite; one stone gave a distinct reading of 1.544, the RI of quartz or chalcedony; other remaining eight samples showed two separate readings of 1.544 and 1.607. These results indicated that the gem material commonly called "sugilite" in the trade actually ranges from relatively pure manganoan sugilite to stones that contain progressively greater amounts of chalcedony. According to the GIA, "samples exhibiting the two refractive indices should not be described as sugilite but rather as a rock consisting of a mixture of sugilite and chalcedony. There is no way to determine if chalcedony is the major constituent of a particular sample by standard

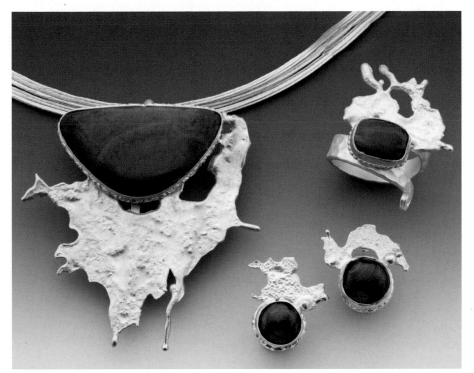

Fig. Su.2 An ensemble of sugilite jewelry by Carina Rossner. *Photo by Randy Polk.*

gemological testing procedures." However, the measurement of specific gravity does provide a rough indication of how much chalcedony a sample of this material might contain, with samples of lower specific gravities containing more chalcedony.

Besides being used for carvings, beads, fantasy cuts, cabochons and faceted stones, sugilite is sometimes inlaid with turquoise, opal, lapis lazuli, rhodochrosite and malachite in decorative objects such as boxes, tables and pendants. Sugilite typically retails from about $5/ct to $200/ct with translucent stones fetching the highest prices and the semi-opaque rock-type sugilites being the least expensive. In general, the greater the translucency and the more intense and even the purple color, the more valuable the gem is. Evenly colored, top-grade translucent sugilite is often called **gem sugilite, gel sugilite** or **AAA gel sugilite**; however, sometimes these names are also applied to average-quality stones, especially on the Internet. Therefore, don't assume that stones sold as gel sugilite are high-grade; buy on the basis of the stone's appearance, rather than on its trade name. Most of the material available on the market today is notably inferior to the sugilite found when the Wessels Mine deposit was first discovered.

The attractiveness of the patterns of mottled stones can also play a role in sugilite pricing. Carvings and sugilite-druse are priced by the piece.

Less expensive material such as lepidolite, dyed jasper, magnesite and plastic are used to imitate sugilite, so be suspicious of bargain priced sugilite. Some genuine sugilite is sold under the trade names "Royal Lavulite" and "Royal Azel." Because of its rarity and unique royal purple color, sugilite is more expensive than many other semi-opaque rock materials. Since it is becoming scarce, the price of sugilite is likely to rise if no new mines are found.

Fig. Su.3 Gem sugilite from South Africa. *Sugilite suite from Pala International; photo by Mia Dixon.*

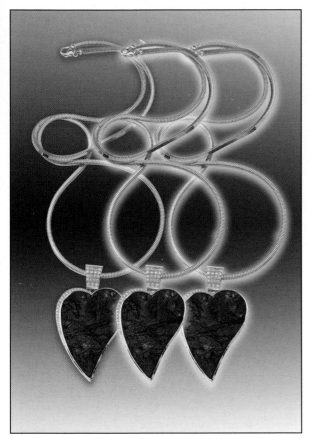

Fig. Su.4 Sugilite pendants by Barbara Westwood. *Photo by Sky Hall.*

Fig. Su.5 Sugilite carving. *Carving and photo from Gerald Stockton. This photo appeared on the cover of the November 1982 issue of* Lapidary Journal.

Fig. Su.6 Gel Sugilite ring by Mark Anderson. *Photo by Jessica Dow.*

Fig. Su.7 Sugilite and rhodolite earrings design © by Eve J. Alfillé. *Photo by Matthew Arden.*

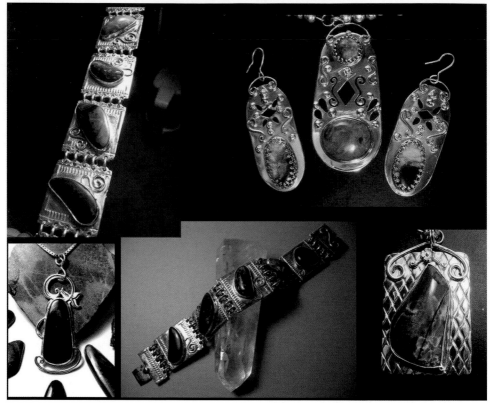

Fig. Su.8 Sugilite jewelry by Jessica Dow of Different Seasons Jewelry. *Photo by Jessica Dow.*

Fig. Su.9 Sugilite pendants by Michael Sugarman. *Photo by Michael Sugarman.*

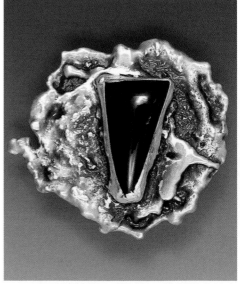

Fig. Su.10 Sugilite pin/pendant. *Jewelry created and photographed by Carina Rossner.*

Unakite (YOU na kite), an altered granite consisting of pink orthoclase feldspar, green epidote and clear quartz

RI: spot readings around 1.74–1.76, 1.55 or 1.52 depending on area tested

Hardness: 6–7	**Luster**: vitreous, greasy, pearly
SG: 2.55–3.20	**Cleavage**: none
Pleochroism: none	**Fracture**: conchoidal, uneven
Toughness: fair	**Crystal form**: none, massive
Fluorescence: usually inert	**Absorption spectrum**: not diagnostic

Stable to light; attacked by hydrofluoric acid; ultrasonic cleaners are usually safe.

Unakite is a pink and green rock, often with white and black specks, which was named for its discovery in the Unaka range of the Great Smoky region of eastern Tennessee and western North Carolina in the United States. Other sources include South Africa, Ontario, Canada and the US states of Virginia and Michigan.

Like most rocks, unakite is inexpensive and sold at costume jewelry prices. It is used for beads, cabochons, freeforms, spheres, pyramids, carvings, containers, and paperweights. Some unakite has been used as tile, e.g., on the main terrace of the National Museum of Natural History (Smithsonian Institution) in Washington, D.C.

For additional information see:
http://www.cst.cmich.edu/users/dietr1rv/unakite.htm

Fig. Un.1 Unakite pendant courtesy Nevada Mineral & Book Co. *Photo © Renée Newman.*

Fig. Un.2 Unakite beads. *Photo © Renée Newman.*

Fig. Un.3 Unakite pendant by Heather B. Moore. *Photo: Heather B. Moore Inc.*

Fig. Un.4 Carved unakite pendant by Amy Kahn Russell. *Photo by Noelle Feucht.*

Vesuvianite (vuh SUE vee an ite) also called **idocrase** (EYE doe craze), silicates class $Ca_{10}(Mg,Fe)_2Al_4(SiO_4)_5(Si_2O_7)_2(OH)_4$, calcium magnesium iron aluminum silicate hydroxide

RI: 1.70-1.72 (spot 1.71)	**Cleavage**: indistinct, rarely seen
Hardness: 6.5	**Luster**: vitreous, greasy;
SG: 3.3–3.5	**Optic char**: DR, uniaxial positive or negative, aggregate
Birefringence: 0.005	**Fracture**: conchoidal, uneven, granular
Dispersion: .019	**Pleochroism**: none to weak
Crystal system: tetragonal	**Crystal shape**: columnar, thick prisms, pyramidal, massive
Toughness: fair to good	**Fluorescence**: usually inert
Magnetism: green – strong	**Treatments**: Normally none except for possible fracture filling

Absorption spectrum: strong band at 464 nm with a weaker band at 528.5 nm
Stable to light; fuses easily with heat; attacked by HCl acid; ultrasonics and steamer are risky.

Vesuvianite was discovered in the 18th century in Naples, Italy at Mount Vesuvius, hence the name given by the German mineralogist Abraham Werner. French mineralogist René Haüy preferred to call it "idocrase," which comes from the Greek words *idos* and *krasis* meaning mixed appearance because idocrase crystals resemble those of other minerals. Both names are still used today, but mineralogists usually call the mineral vesuvianite, and consider "idocrase" a synonym.

Transparent green to green-yellow vesuvianite is currently the most widely available variety of this mineral. Magadi, Kenya has the highest commercial production of the material. Retail prices of transparent vesuvianite run roughly $15/ct–$80/ct depending on size and quality.

The Jeffrey Quarry in Asbestos, Quebec has produced vesuvianite in a variety of colors— yellowish green, chrome-green, purple, pink, and brown. Beautiful transparent green and brown vesuvianite is also found in Laurel, Quebec. Production is not even close to that of the Kenyan locality, prompting collectors to pay a higher price for the Canadian gems if locality is an important factor in their collecting program.

Another variety of vesuvianite, which is bright green to yellow-green and translucent to semi-opaque, is named **californite**. According to Joel Arem's *Color Encyclopedia of Gemstones* (p 116), "Californite is a massive idocrase-grossular mixture reported first from California and later found in various other localities such as Africa and Pakistan." Since californite resembles jade, it has erroneously been called California jade or American jade. The semi-opaque material is typically used for beads and carvings while the higher quality translucent material is used for cabochons and occasionally faceted stones. Retail prices for the higher qualities of californite are in the $40/ct–$50/ct range.

Fig. Ve.1 Californite. *Coast-to-Coast Rarestones International.*

Norway is known for a rare light blue variety of vesuvianite called **cyprine**. It is an important gem in the collector's market but has little use in jewelry. Other sources of vesuvianite include Tanzania, Italy, Russia, and the northeastern United States.

The *GIA Gem Identification Lab Manual* (2005) (p 226) says that "jadeite-like idocrase is often mixed with hydrogrossular, so it might be impossible to separate the two species." Vesuvianite can also be confused with serpentine, nephrite, zoisite, diopside and peridot.

Fig. Ve.2 Vesuvianite earrings created by Amy Kahn Russell. *Photo by Noelle Feucht.*

Fig. Ve.3 Vesuvianite earrings created by Amy Kahn Russell. *Photo by Noelle Feucht.*

Fig. Ve.4 Vesuvianite crystals (Jeffrey Quarry, Asbestos, Quebec, Canada). *Specimen & photo from Rob Lavinsky of The Arkenstone.*

Fig. Ve.5 Purple mangan-vesuvianite (Jeffrey Quarry, Asbestos, Quebec, Canada). *Specimen & photo from Rob Lavinsky of The Arkenstone.*

Fig. Ve.6 Chrome vesuvianite (Jeffrey Mine Asbestos, Quebec, Canada). *Specimen and photo from Rob Lavinsky of The Arkenstone.*

Fig. Ve.7 Wine-red vesuvianite from Bellecombe, Italy. *Courtesy Rob Lavinsky of The Arkenstone.*

Fig. Ve.8 Canadian vesuvianite pendant. *Crafted and photographed by Carina Rossner.*

Fig. Ve.9 Vesuvianite earrings. *Crafted and photographed by Carina Rossner.*

Fig. Ve. 10 Vesuvianite from Magadi, Kenya. *Coast to Coast Rarestones International.*

Fig. Ve.11 Vesuvianite from Laurel, Quebec. *Coast-to-Coast Rarestones International.*

Fig. Ve.12 Vesuvianite cabs from Magadi, Kenya. *Courtesy Coast to Coast Rarestones International.*

Fig. Ve.13 Vesuvianite beads from Italy courtesy Mary & Leslie D'Souza of Beads Direct. *Photo © Renée Newman.*

Rare Gems Sometimes Used in Jewelry

Amblygonite (am BLIG oh nite), phosphates class, amblygonite group
Based on Raman tests by Stone Group Labs, most of the facet-grade material is in the montebrasite range of the amblygonite series, but the trade normally calls it "amblygonite." Chemical formula: $(Li,Na)Al(PO_4)(F,OH)$, Lithium sodium aluminum phosphate fluoride hydroxide

RI: 1.612–1.636   **Cleavage**: perfect in one direction, good in one direction
Hardness: 5.5–6   **Luster**: vitreous, pearly
SG: 2.98–3.06   **Optic char**: DR biaxial positive or negative
Birefringence: .020–.027   **Fracture**: conchoidal, uneven
Dispersion: .018   **Pleochroism**: weak to none
Crystal system: triclinic   **Crystal shape**: prismatic, tabular, granular, massive
Toughness: poor   **Absorption spectrum**: not diagnostic
Magnetism: nonmagnetic   **Treatments**: frequently irradiated to turn the color green, blue or a stronger yellow
Fluorescence: very weak green or orange (LW), light blue phosphorescence (LW and SW)
Stable to light; very sensitive to heat; cracks when heated unevenly; attacked by many acids. Avoid ultrasonic and steam cleaners. Warm soapy water is safe.

First discovered in 1817 in Saxony Germany, amblygonite is typically white, colorless or light yellow, but it can be irradiated to produce various shades of green and occasionally blue. According to Cara Williams of Stone Group Labs, irradiated amblygonite is stable in sunlight, but fades to its original color upon heating. The irradiated material they tested was all pinkish under the Chelsea color filter. After heating back to natural color, the pink was no longer visible, so it seems a direct effect of the change due to irradiation. Treated colors seen by the Stone Group Labs include a yellow-green similar to chrysoberyl, a light lemon yellow similar to lighter yellow sapphire, and a blue-green similar to an unheated aqua, in addition to light blue and light green.

Most amblygonite today comes from Brazil, but Spain, Myanmar and California in the United States are also sources. It is commonly found in the same mines as apatite, lepidolite, quartz, spodumene and tourmaline.

Amblygonite is usually transparent to semitransparent and eye-clean, so it is normally faceted. However, because of its cleavage, the gem is seldom set in rings. It is more practical for pendants, earrings, brooches and mineral collections. Retail prices range from about $30/ct–$90/ct. Most stones are less than 15 carats, but stones above 50 carats have also been cut. Besides being mounted in jewelry and purchased by mineral collectors, amblygonite is an important source of lithium and phosphorous for industry.

Fig. Amb.1 Amblygonite. *Photo and gem from Coast-to-Coast Rarestones.*

Fig. Amb.2 Amblygonite from D & J Rare Gems. *Photo by Donna Rhoads.*

Axinite (AK sin ite), silicates class, axinite group
Chemical formula: $(Ca, Fe, Mn, Mg)_3Al_2BSi_4O_{15}(OH)$ calcium aluminum borosilicate hydroxide of magnesium, iron or manganese

RI: 1.674–1.704
Hardness: 6.5–7
SG: 3.26–3.36
Birefringence: .010–.012
Dispersion: .018–.020
Crystal system: triclinic
Luster: greasy to vitreous
Toughness: fair to poor
Magnetism: drags

Cleavage: distinct in one direction, poor in others
Fracture: conchoidal to uneven
Optic char: DR, biaxial negative
Pleochroism: strong violet to purple, light yellow and red-brown
Fluorescence: usually inert, yellow stones may fluoresce red (SW)
Crystal shape: wedge-shaped, flattened ax-head shaped
Absorption spectrum: lines at 412, 466, 492 and 512 nm
Treatments: normally none; fracture-filling is possible
Stable to light; sensitive to heat; not attacked by chemicals

Named after the axe shape of its crystals, axinite is usually brown and often transparent, but it is occasionally yellow, lavender, blue or orange. Axinite's strong trichroism is a distinguishing feature which sometimes creates flashes of more than one color face up. Cut stones above five carats are rare. Retails prices are roughly $15/ct–$100/ct and sometimes as much as $200/ct.

Two major sources of axinite are Mexico, which produces mostly brown material, and Tanzania, where yellow, lavender and blue crystals are sometimes found. Other axinite localities include Russia, France, England, Switzerland, Brazil, Japan, Pakistan and the United States.

Fig. Ax.1 Pleochroism visible in pavilion view of an axinite from Pakistan. *The Arkenstone.*

Fig. Ax.2 Mexican axinite (4.98 ct). *Gem & photo from Coast-to-Coast Rarestones.*

Fig. Ax.3 Mexican axinite (3.62 ct) accented by hessonite garnets in a ring by D & J Rare Gems. *Photo by Donna Rhoads.*

Fig. Ax.4 Tanzanian axinite. *Crystal & photo from Rob Lavinsky of The Arkenstone.*

Fig. Ax.5 Axinite crystals from Switzerland on matrix. *Specimen & photo: The Arkenstone.*

Brazilianite (bra ZIL ya nite), phosphates class
Chemical formula: $NaAl_3(PO_4)_2(OH)_4$, sodium aluminum phosphate hydroxide

RI: 1.60–1.636	**Cleavage**: good in one direction
Hardness: 5.5	**Luster**: vitreous
SG: 2.94–3.00	**Optic char**: DR, biaxial positive
Birefringence: .019–.021	**Fracture**: conchoidal
Dispersion: .014	**Pleochroism**: very weak
Crystal system: monoclinic	**Crystal form**: prismatic, wedge-shaped, rounded
Toughness: poor to fair	**Absorption spectrum**: not diagnostic
Fluorescence: inert	**Treatments**: usually none

Stable to light; sensitive to heat; may lose color; slowly attacked by acids; ultrasonics are risky.

Named for Brazil, the country in which it was discovered in 1944, brazilianite is a rare yellow-green gem, which is often transparent and eye-clean, except in large sizes. It may also be yellow, white or colorless. Occasionally it is mounted in jewelry, but most of it is bought by collectors. According to John Bradshaw of Coast-to-Coast Rarestones International, most fine, smaller brazilianites retail between $60/ct–$100/ct and larger, fine stones should retail between $200/ct–$600/ct. Exceptional stones might cost more. Almost all of the brazilianite on the market is from Brazil. However, rare specimens have also been found in New Hampshire in the United States and in the Yukon, Canada.

Fig. Br.2 Brazilianite. *Gem and photo courtesy Coast-to-Coast Rarestones Intl.*

Fig. Br.1 Brazilianite rough and faceted stone from Brazil cut by Clay Zava of Zava Mastercuts. *Photo by Robert & Orasa Weldon.*

Fig. Br.3 Brazilianite from Rapid Creek, Yukon, Canada. *Specimen & photo from Rob Lavinsky of The Arkenstone.*

Cuprite (KOO prite) oxides class
Chemical formula: Cu_2O, copper oxide

RI: 2.848–2.850	**Cleavage**: imperfect, usually not visible
Hardness: 3.5–4	**Luster**: adamantine, submetallic, earthy
SG: 6.00–6.15	**Optic char**: SR
Birefringence: none	**Fracture**: conchoidal, uneven
Pleochroism: anomalous	**Absorption spectrum**: not diagnostic
Crystal system: cubic	**Crystal form**: cube, octahedron, dodecahedron, massive, crust, grains
Toughness: poor	**Fluorescence**: inert

Treatments: Normally none for crystalline material. Massive (non-crystalline) cuprite is sometimes coated with colorless wax, or occasionally impregnated with plastic and/or other agents to improve durability and appearance.

Color is stable to light, but a surface film can form with long exposure to strong light; fuses to jeweler's torch; soluble in nitric acid and hydrochloric acid. Weathering and oxidation can cause cuprite crystals to turn gradually into malachite over the years. Avoid ultrasonic cleaners.

Cuprite crystals are various shades of red to dark red. In reflected light, they may sometimes look nearly black, but in transmitted light, they can be a gorgeous Mogok ruby red. In addition, they are noted for their high brilliance. Massive semi-opaque cuprite is reddish orange to brownish orange and sometimes forms a pretty orange, blue-green, and black rock with chrysocolla and tenorite; it has the trade name **Sonora Sunrise** or **Sonora Sunrise chrysocolla** because much of it is found in the state of Sonora in Mexico. When the stone has no chrysocolla and is only orange and black, some vendors call it **Sonoran Sunrise cuprite**.

Cuprite, which is an ore of copper, derives its name from the Latin *cuprum* for "copper." It is typically found in desert areas in oxidized zones of copper mines. Sources include Namibia, Mexico, Australia, Bolivia, France, the Ural Mountains, the Congo, and the states of Arizona, New Mexico and Utah in the U. S.

Even though cuprite is relatively soft, crystalline material is faceted and sold to collectors. It is occasionally mounted in jewelry, such as pendants and earrings, but is not recommended as a ring stone. The largest cuprite on record is probably a 647-carat stone cut by Michael Gray. Faceted cuprites generally retail from around $50/ct –$120/ct. You can find nice Sonoran Sunrise cabochons for less than $100. However, many of the most attractive stones are purchased by designers and mounted in creative jewelry. Expect to pay more for one-of-a-kind pieces than for mass-produced jewelry.

Cuprite must be stored away from strong light because prolonged exposure to light may cause the formation of a green patina on its surface. This thin film is malachite, which through oxidation can eventually replace the structure of the cuprite.

Fig. Cu.1 Cuprite ring. *Jewelry and photo by Carina Rossner.*

Fig. Cu.2 Namibian cuprite (46.07 ct) from Pala International. *Photo by Mia Dixon.*

Fig. Cu.3 Barbara Westwood's Sedona Collection featuring Mexican cuprite and other gems including hematite, chrysocolla, blue opal and turquoise. *Photo by Sky Hall.*

Fig. Cu.4 Sonoran Sunrise bracelet by Susan Sadler. *Photo by Jeffrey Mobley.*

Fig. Cu.5 Sonoran Sunrise bracelet by Susan Sadler. *Photo by Jeffrey Mobley.*

Fig. Cu.6 Cuprite crystal from Chessy, France that has turned into malachite through oxidation. *Specimen and photo from Rob Lavinsky of The Arkenstone.*

Fig. Cu.7 Cuprite gem-grade crystal from Red Dome Mine, Chillagoe, Queensland, Australia viewed with backlighting. *Specimen from Rob Lavinsky of The Arkenstone: Joe Budd Photos.*

Epidote (EPP ih dote) a minerals species in the epidote group and silicates class
Chemical formula: $Ca_2(Al,Fe)_3(SiO_4)_3(OH)$, calcium aluminum iron silicate hydroxide

RI: 1.729–1.768   **Cleavage**: perfect in one direction lengthwise
Hardness: 6–7   **Luster**: vitreous, greasy
SG: 3.30–3.50   **Optic char**: DR, biaxial negative
Birefringence: .019–.048   **Fracture**: conchoidal, uneven
Dispersion: .030   **Pleochroism**: strong green, brown and yellow
Crystal system: monoclinic **Crystal form**: long slender prisms, crusts, tabular, massive
Toughness: fair to poor   **Magnetism**: usually magnetic
Fluorescence: usually inert **Treatments**: normally none, fracture filling possible
Absorption spectrum: strong band at 455 nm and sometimes weak line at 475 nm.
Stable to light; fusible to heat; partly decomposed by some acids; ultrasonics are risky.

Epidote is typically green, brown or black and translucent to transparent. The green is sometimes described as pistachio or avocado-colored, but most green epidote is so dark that it looks forest green or black. Facet-quality material is mined primarily in Brazil, but is also found in Austria, Pakistan, Sri Lanka, Tanzania and Alaska in the United States. Other sources of epidote include Mexico, Italy, India, Russia and Mozambique.

Epidote is the primary component of **unakite**, a green and pink rock used for beads, cabochons and ornaments. Quartz and prehnite with epidote inclusions are sometimes used in jewelry and are sold as epidote quartz or prehnite and epidote. Faceted stones are rare and usually sold to collectors; they retail for around $20/ct–$80/ct.

Figs. Ep.1 & 2 A Sri Lankan epidote (left) and Pakistani epidotes (right). *Gemstones & photo from Coast-to-Coast Rarestones International.*

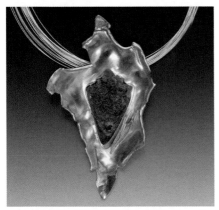

Fig. Ep.3 Epidote druse pendant. *Crafted and photographed by Carina Rossner.*

Fig. Ep.4 Epidote and prehnite pendant. *Jewelry and photo by Carina Rossner.*

Haüyne (pronounced "how EEN"), **Hauyne** or **Hauynite**, silicates class, sodalite group $(Na,Ca)_{4-8}(AlSiO_4)_6(SO_4,)_{1-2}$ (formula from Dana's *Manual of Mineralogy),* complex sodium aluminum silicate, a component of lapis lazuli

RI: 1.494-1.505   **Cleavage**: distinct in one direction
Hardness: 5.5-6   **Luster**: vitreous to greasy
SG: 2.4–2.5   **Fracture**: uneven or conchoidal
Birefringence: none   **Absorption spectrum**: not diagnostic
Dispersion: low   **Crystal form**: dodecahedral or rounded
Crystal system: cubic   **Treatments**: fracture filling is possible
Optic char: isotropic   Stable to light, soluble in acids, clean in warm soapy water
Fluorescence: usually none; may show an orangy pink under LW

   Top quality haüyne has good transparency and a beautiful intense blue color even in small sizes less than .05 ct. Named for René Just Haüy, a French pioneer in crystallography, it was first described in 1807 from crystals at the Mount Somma Vesuvius volcano in Italy. The finest material is found in the Eifel Mountains of Germany. Other less significant sources include Afghanistan, Australia, Canada, Russia, China and the USA.

   Although typically blue, haüyne may also be greenish blue, green, white, gray, yellow or pink, and its transparency can range from transparent to semi-opaque. Haüyne crystals are very rare and small—about 1-2 mm in size. Melee 0.05 ct or less can retail for up to $500/ct. Stones between 0.05 and 0.15 ct can cost up to $1000/ct. The number of stones larger than 0.15 ct are very limited with prices ranging from around $1200/ct-$7000/ct depending on size and quality. Fine stones above one carat are virtually unobtainable on a regular basis and are priced as such. Low grade material with poor transparency sells for much less, but in general, haüyne is one of the highest priced rare gems.

Figs. Ha.1–3 Haüyne crystals and stones. *Cut & photographed by Coast-to-Coast Rarestones.*

Fig. Ha.4 Haüyne (.83 ct) from Mayer & Watt. *Photo by Geoffrey Watt.*   **Fig. Ha.5** Haüyne. *Specimen and photo from Rob Lavinsky of The Arkenstone.*

Hemimorphite (hem ih MORE fite), silicates class
Chemical formula: $Zn_4Si_2O_7(OH)_2.H_2O$, hydrated zinc silicate hydroxide

RI: 1.614-1.636	**Cleavage**: perfect in 1 direction, poor in 1direction
Hardness: 4.5–5	**Luster**: vitreous, silky, pearly, dull
SG: 3.4–3.5	**Optic char**: DR, biaxial positive, aggregate
Birefringence: .022	**Fracture**: uneven to conchoidal
Dispersion: none	**Pleochroism**: none to weak
Crystal system: orthorhombic	**Crystal shape**: bladed, botryoidal, massive
Toughness: poor	**Fluorescence**: usually inert

Absorption spectra: not diagnostic Strongly pyroelectric and piezoelectric
Treatments: occasionally dyed, commonly stabilized with wax or polymers
Stable to light; very sensitive to heat; gelatinizes easily with acids; avoid ultrasonics.

Most hemimorphite is translucent and blue to green or white, but it may also be brown, gray or yellow and is occasionally banded. Turquoise-colored stones are sometimes confused with smithsonite or turquoise. Transparent colorless hemimorphite is found almost exclusively in Mapimi, Durango or Santa Eulalia, Chihuahua in Mexico; it rarely exceeds two carats in size and can retail for as much as $300/ct if it is of high clarity. Heavily included material will sell for much less. Blue massive material is generally used for cutting cabochons and tends to be in the $10/ct–$20/ct range. Some very intense blue Chinese translucent material has sold for up to $150/ct retail. Drusy blue hemimorphite is generally priced by the piece.

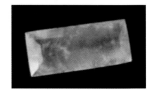

Fig. He.1 Congo hemimorphite. *The Arkenstone.*

Hemimorphite means "half formed," in reference to the contrasting terminations at opposite ends of a crystal; one end is like a pyramid and the other is blunt. A unique characteristic of the mineral is that a state of temporary electrical polarization is produced by a change in temperature (pyroelectricity) or pressure (piezoelectricity), which attracts dust and dirt and requires hemimorphite to be cleaned on a regular basis.

Fig. He.2 Cadmium hemimorphite. *The Arkenstone.*

Other localities besides Mexico include the Congo, China, Namibia, Zambia, Australia, Siberia, Germany, Romania, Greece, Italy and the United States.

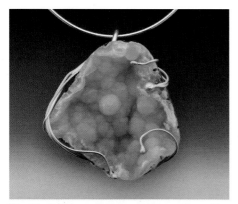

Fig. He.3 Chinese hemimorphite pendant. *Created and photographed by Carina Rossner.*

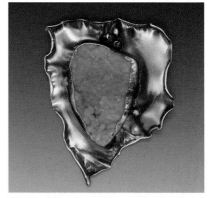

Fig. He.4 Hemimorphite pendant by Carina Rossner. *Photo by George Post.*

Jeremejevite (YE re me YAY vite), borates class, $Al_6B_5O_{15}(F,OH)_3$, aluminum borate

RI: 1.630–1.653
Hardness: 7
SG: 3.27–3.31
Birefringence: .013
Dispersion: .013
Luster: vitreous
Toughness: good
Fluorescence: none

Cleavage: none
Crystal system: hexagonal or orthorhombic
Fracture: conchoidal
Absorption spectrum: vague absorption band at about 5000
Pleochroism: blue/colorless to light yellow in Namibian material
Crystal form: prismatic, elongated pyramidal, small grains
Treatments: normally none, fracture filling possible
Stable to light: usually not heat sensitive

Optic char: DR, biaxial or uniaxial negative depending on how the crystal grows. For example, specimens from Russia may have uniaxial rims but biaxial cores; biaxial rims with uniaxial cores are sometimes observed in Namibian material (*Color Encyclopedia of Gemstones,* Joel Arem). Jeremejevite is piezoelectric—it generates an electric charge when mechanical pressure is applied.

If you find aquamarine appealing, you'll probably like Namibian jeremejevite. It is usually light to medium-light blue and may be greenish or violetish, although it is occasionally colorless or brownish yellow. First found in Siberia in the late nineteenth century, jeremejevite was named after Pavel Vladimirovich Jeremejev (1830–1899), the Russian mineralogist and crystallographer who first recognized the species.

Namibia is the source of almost all of the faceted jeremejevites on the market. Most of it is blue, and eye-visible inclusions are common, but a fine brilliant cut can help mask the inclusions. The crystals tend to be extremely elongated and narrow so faceted jeremejevites are often elongated rectangles. Recently, colorless stones as large as 60 carats have come from Madagascar, and some colorless jeremejevites are attributed to Zambia. Other minor localities are Russia, Tajikistan, Myanmar and Germany.

Because of its beauty, rarity and durability, jeremejevite is an expensive gem that is highly sought after by collectors. In sizes below one carat, jeremejevite generally retails for between $200/ct–$1500/ct with well-cut, eye-clean blue stones fetching the highest prices. Retail prices for blue stones 1-carat and above are roughly $400/ct–$4000/ct. Bill Larson of Pala International says that there is also light yellow jeremejevite from Mogok, Myanmar, which sells for about $100-1000/ct in the 1–4 carat range. Even though jeremejevites make attractive jewelry, most are sold to collectors because of their scarcity.

Figs. Je.1–Je.3 Namibian jeremejevites. *Courtesy of Coast to Coast Rarestones International.*

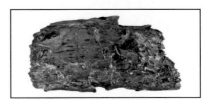

Fig. Je.4 Namibian jeremejevite. *Courtesy Coast-to-Coast Rarestones.*

Fig. Je.5 Namibian jeremejevite. *Crystal and photo from The Arkenstone.*

Kornerupine (korn eh ROO peen), silicates class

Chemical formula: $Mg_3AL_6(SI,Al,B)_5O_{21}(OH)$, Hydrous magnesium aluminum borosilicate

RI: 1.66-1.68
Hardness: 6.5–7
SG: 3.28–3.35
Birefringence: .012–.017
Dispersion: .019
Crystal system: orthorhombic

Cleavage: perfect in two directions
Luster: vitreous
Optic char: DR, biaxial negative
Fracture: conchoidal
Crystal shape: elongated prisms and rounded grains
Toughness: fair to poor

Trichroism: generally strong green, yellow, and red-brown
Fluorescence: inert to strong yellow under LW and SW;
Spectrum: bands at 446 nm and 503 nm; faint lines at 430 nm, 463 nm, and 540 nm
Treatments: normally not treated except for possible fracture filling
Stable to light; insoluble in acids; ultrasonics are risky, warm soapy water is safe.

Named after the Danish geologist Andreas Nikolaus Kornerup (1857-1883), kornerupine was discovered in Fiskenaesset, Greenland in 1884. It can be green, yellow-green, blue-green, brownish green, brown, yellow, pink, lavender, purple or colorless. Translucent varieties may show chatoyancy or asterism.

Sri Lanka, Madagascar and Tanzania are the most important sources, but kornerupine is also found in Kenya, Australia, Greenland and Myanmar. Tanzanian material is noted for its blue-green color.

According to John Bradshaw of Coast-to-Coast Rarestones, brown kornerupines in sizes up to 5 carats typically retail for $20/ct-$200/ct, the more expensive reserved for the finer stones; a few larger browns are available from time to time at a higher cost. Brighter color greens, purples, blue-greens are mostly from Tanzania and more often than not are less than 1 carat; they can retail for up to $500/ct. Fine stones over 1 carat will be higher.

Fig. Ko.1 Sri Lankan kornerupine from D & J Rare Gems. *Photo: D. Rhoads.*

Fig. Ko.2 Sri Lankan kornerupine cat's-eye from D & J Rare Gems. *Photo: D. Rhoads.*

Fig. Ko.3 Sri Lankan kornerupine from Pala International. *Photo by Mia Dixon.*

Fig. Ko.4 Tanzanian kornerupine. *Rough and photo from New Era Gems.*

Lepidolite (Li PID l ite), silicates class, mica group
Formula: $K(Li,Al)_3(Si,Al)_4O_{10}(F,OH)_2$, hydrous potassium lithium aluminum silicate

RI: 1.53–1.556	**Cleavage**: perfect in one direction
Hardness: 2.5–4	**Luster**: sub-vitreous to pearly
SG: 2.8–3.3	**Optic char**: DR, biaxial negative, aggregate
Birefringence: .026	**Pleochroism**: none
Dispersion: none	**Fracture**: uneven
Crystal system: monoclinic	**Crystal shape**: massive, tabular, short prismatic
Fluorescence: inert	Stable to light; fuses easily; insoluble in acid.

Treatments: can be impregnated with wax or resins to improve durability; avoid ultrasonics

Lepidolite, the most common lithium-bearing mineral, typically has a lavender color, but it may also be pink, purple, white, gray or yellow. It is usually translucent to semi-opaque; however, transparent to semi-transparent crystals are also found. Its name originates from the Greek *lepido* meaning "scale" and *lithos* "stone" because of the scaly appearance of lepidolite rock.

San Diego County, California, in the U.S. and Minas Gerais, Brazil are the two most important lepidolite localities, with Brazil producing the finest crystals, some of which have been faceted. However, San Diego County is noted for having produced the largest quantity. Other sources of lepidolite include Madagascar, Mozambique, Namibia, Zimbabwe, Japan, the Czech Republic, Afghanistan and the Ural Mountains of Russia. Lepidolite is commonly found in mines with tourmaline, kunzite, beryl and quartz.

Lepidolite is extremely important for its industrial applications because of its lithium content. This element is used for rechargeable long-life lithium batteries, antidepressant medication, lubricants, air-conditioning systems and thermal shock-resistant glass such as Pyrex and Corningware. When combined with aluminum, lithium creates a lightweight strong aerospace alloy. Lithium is predicted to be the premium fuel in the future for generating pollution-free electricity in fusion reactors; liquid lithium metal's high specific heat capacity and low melting point make it the best coolant for such reactors. Consequently, lepidolite is in high demand by industry.

Lepidolite is also used for ornamental purposes such as bookends, paperweights, spheres, figurines and jewelry. Strands of promotional quality beads with many dark and white inclusions sell for as little as $2 per strand. However, the price goes up as the color becomes more even and saturated, and as the transparency increases. High-quality strands can retail for a few hundred dollars. Lepidolite is also used to make attractive pendants and earrings, which can be conversation pieces because of all the unique uses of the stone.

Some folks say that their skin is greatly smoothed by putting lepidolite into bath water, and it is used by a few cosmetic companies, possibly for that reason.

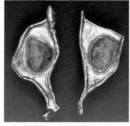

Figs. Lep.1 & 2 Lepidolite pendant & earrings. *Crafted and photographed by Carina Rossner.*   **Fig. Lep.3** Brazilian lepidolite. *Crystals and photo from The Arkenstone.*

Phenakite (FEN a kite), silicates class, phenakite group
Chemical formula: Be_2SiO_4, beryllium silicate

RI: 1.654–1.670	**Cleavage**: indistinct in one direction
Hardness: 7.5–8	**Luster**: vitreous
SG: 2.95–3.00	**Optic char**: DR, uniaxial positive
Birefringence: .016	**Crystal system**: hexagonal (trigonal)
Dispersion: .015	**Pleochroism**: moderate to weak in colored crystals
Toughness: good	**Absorption spectrum**: not diagnostic
Fracture: conchoidal	**Crystal shape**: prismatic, rhombohedral, granular
Treatments: normally none	Stable to light; infusible to heat; not attacked by acids

Fluorescence: inert to weak pink, light blue or green (LW and SW); ultrasonics usually safe

If you'd like an affordable diamond substitute that is bright, durable and completely natural, consider buying a phenakite. Although it can be pink, light yellow, brownish, or white, much of the phenakite entering the market now is colorless and transparent. It was named in 1833 from the Greek for "deceiver" because it was often mistaken for quartz.

Phenakite is found in the Ural Mountains of Russia, the Pikes Peak region of Colorado (USA), Minas Gerais, Brazil, Norway, Myanmar, Namibia, Madagascar and Nigeria. It is usually faceted or sold as mineral specimens. Transparent eye-clean stones generally retail for between $60/ct–$120/ct and are typically in the 1–5 carat range. Though very rare, phenakite is becoming more available thanks to new finds in Africa.

Fig. Ph.1 Phenakite (6.15 ct) ring by Gordon Aatlo. *Photo by Kelly Allen.*

Fig. Ph.2 Russian Urals phenakite. *From Coast-to-Coast Rare Gems International.*

Fig. Ph.3 Phenakite from Jos, Plateau State, Nigeria. *Specimen and photo from Rob Lavinsky of The Arkenstone.*

Fig. Ph.4 Phenakite crystal from Minas Gerais, Brazil. *Specimen and photo from Rob Lavinsky of The Arkenstone.*

Scapolite (SCAP oh lite), a mineral group consisting of marialite $Na_4Al_3Si_9O_{24}Cl$, meionite $Ca_4Al_6Si_6O_{24}(CO_3)$ and silvialite $Ca_4Al_6Si_6O_{24}(SO_4)$, members of the silicates class. The term "scapolite" is used for all gemstones in the scapolite group because it is not possible to identify the individual members without a chemical analysis.

Luster: vitreous	**RI**: 1.54–1.58 (the higher the calcium content the higher the RI)
Hardness: 6–6.5	**Cleavage**: distinct in two directions
SG: 2.50–2.78	**Optic char**: DR, uniaxial negative
Birefringence: .009–.026	**Fracture**: conchoidal, subconchoidal, uneven, splintery
Dispersion: .017	**Fluorescence**: inert to strong pink, orange, or yellow (LW & SW)
Crystal system: tetragonal	**Crystal shape**: prismatic, massive **Toughness**: fair

Absorption spectrum: purple and violet—663 and 652 nm lines, total absorption below 410 nm.
Pleochroism: pink to violet—strong, dark blue and lavender blue; yellow—weak to moderate, yellow and pale yellow or colorless.
Treatments: Irradiation to produce purple from colorless or yellow; fracture-filling is possible. Stable to light except for irradiated stones which fade rapidly; fuses easily; attacked by acids.

Scapolite is often confused with amethyst and citrine quartz because of its similar refractive index, density and colors. However, scapolite can be more expensive because of its rarity. High quality transparent scapolite has been found in many countries including Myanmar, Sri Lanka, Tanzania, Brazil, Afghanistan and Canada. Yellow scapolite, the most common color, is readily available in sizes up to 10 carats and is now primarily mined in Tanzania. Natural-color purple to violet scapolite is rapidly decreasing in availability, particularly in sizes above 3 carats; it sells for more than yellow material. Tanzania used to be the main source of purple scapolite but now the bulk is from Badakhshan, Afghanistan in sizes mostly of 1 carat or less. Colorless to yellow scapolite can be irradiated to produce a purple color but since irradiated stones often have brown overtones and their color is not stable, scapolites are not commonly irradiated.

Colorless stones are usually from Sri Lanka or Myanmar as well as from a 2005 find in Afghanistan. The latter produces colorless material that fluoresces bright orange-yellow under long-wave UV radiation and shows a blue tenebrescence after exposure to short-wave UV radiation. **Tenebrescence** is the ability of certain materials to darken in response to radiation of one wavelength and then reversibly lighten on exposure to a different wavelength. This property can be observed with sunglasses that darken when you go outdoors in sunlight.

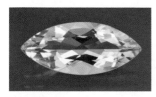

Figs. Sca.1 & 2 Tenebrescent Tajikistan scapolite (3.44 ct) before (left) and after (right) temporary exposure to SW UV light. *Scapolite courtesy Pala International; Mia Dixon.*

John Bradshaw of Coast-to-Coast Rarestones International says that a new source in Nunavut, Canada is producing a light yellow to colorless scapolite that fluoresces so intensely under LW radiation that it can be viewed without dimming any room lighting. Some of the Canadian stones also show tenebrescence. General retail prices for scapolite are shown below. Prices for very large stones are negotiable.

Yellow scapolites:	1 to 10 ct	$10/ct–$100/ct		
Purple scapolites:	.5 to 1 ct	$40/ct–$120/ct	1 to 3 ct	$60/ct–$200/ct
Colorless (tenebrescent):	<1 ct	$200/ct–$500/ct	1 ct to 1.50 ct	$500/ct–$800/ct
Canadian fluorescent & tenebrescent: $100/ct–$200/ct				

Cat's-eye scapolite is available in pink, purple, brown, yellow, gray or white, and originates from a variety of sources including Myanmar, Sri Lanka, India, Brazil, Madagascar and Tajikistan. The retail price range is wide—from around $5/ct for some Indian cat's-eye scapolites to as much as $200/ct for stones from Tajikistan and Canada. According to Bill Larson of Pala International, the finest purple Burmese cat's-eyes can cost $1000/ct even in Burma. Star scapolites from Sri Lanka are also available but rare.

Fig. Sca.3 Tanzanian scapolite (2.95 ct). *Cut & photographed by Robert Drummond of Mountain Lily Gems.*

Fig. Sca.4 Tanzanian scapolite (2.02 ct). *Gem and photo courtesy New Era Gems.*

Fig. Sca.5 Indian scapolite (30.15 ct). *Gem and photo courtesy John S. White.*

Fig. Sca.6 Scapolite. *Gem rough and photo courtesy of New Era Gems.*

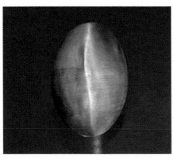

Fig. Sca.7 Cat's-eye scapolite (8.82 ct) from Tajikistan. *Gem from Pala International; photo by Mia Dixon.*

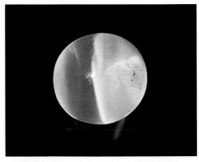

Fig. Sca.8 Cat's-eye scapolite (16.15 ct) from Mogok, Myanmar. *Gemstone from Pala International; photo by Mia Dixon.*

Scheelite (SHE lite), sulfates class, scheelite group
Chemical formula: $CaWO_4$, calcium tungstate

RI: 1.915–1.937	**Cleavage**: distinct in one direction
Hardness: 4.5–5	**Luster**: subadamantine
SG: 5.90–6.12	**Optic char**: DR, uniaxial positive
Birefringence: .016	**Fracture**: subconchoidal to uneven
Dispersion: .038	**Pleochroism**: weak in orange stones
Toughness: poor	**Absorption spectrum**: 584 nm doublet in orange stones
Crystal system: tetragonal	**Crystal shape**: pseudooctahedral, bipyramidal, massive, granular

Fluorescence: inert (LW); colorless gems—strong light blue (SW); orange gems—yellowish (SW).
Treatments: normally not treated. Stable to light; almost infusible; attacked by acids

Faceted scheelites are sometimes mistaken for yellow diamonds because of their diamond-like fire, high brilliance and luster. In fact, they are even synthesized to imitate diamond. Although most faceted scheelites are yellow to orange-yellow, some are colorless, orange, brown or greenish brown and range from transparent to translucent. Named after Swedish chemist Karl Wilhelm Scheele, the discoverer of tungsten, scheelite is a chief ore of tungsten. It is an important metal for rockets, industrial tools and electric light filaments because it has the highest melting point (3,422° C) and lowest thermal expansion of any pure metal. A distinguishing characteristic of scheelite is its strong bright sky-blue glow under shortwave UV light. Prospectors use this fluorescence not only to search for scheelite but to also locate gold, often an associated mineral.

Most of the faceted scheelite currently on the market is from China. According to John Bradshaw of Coast-to-Coast Rarestones International, the next most common scheelite after the Chinese is the colorless material from Kern County, California. Other sources include Brazil, Mexico, Sri Lanka, Romania, Australia, Korea and Russia. Faceted scheelite retails at about $15/ct for heavily included, translucent material to about $80/ct for well-cut moderately included material and $80/ct–$300/ct for transparent eye-clean stones up to 20 carats. Larger stones will demand more per carat as the amount of available rough is dwindling.

Fig. Sc.1 Sri Lankan scheelite. *Gem and photo from Coast-to-Coast Rarestones.*

Fig. Sc.2 Sri Lankan star scheelite from D & J Rare Gems. *Photo by D. Rhoads.*

Fig. Sc.3 Chinese scheelite (35.35 ct). *Courtesy Robert Drummond of Mountain Lily Gems.*

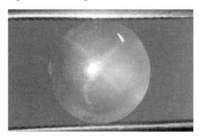

Fig. Sc.4 Chinese scheelite (17.85 ct). *Courtesy Coast-to-Coast Rarestones.*

Sillimanite (SILL i ma nite), silicates class; andalusite group
Chemical formula: Al_2SiO_5, aluminum silicate. Kyanite and andalusite have the same
chemical composition as sillimanite, but different crystal structures

RI: 1.657–1.680	**Cleavage**: perfect in one direction, making it difficult to cut
Birefringence: .015–.021	**Hardness**: 7.5, but 6–7 for fibrous material
SG: 3.14–3.25	**Luster**: silky when fibrous, vitreous otherwise
Dispersion: .015	**Optic char**: DR biaxial positive, AGG
Fracture: splintery, uneven	**Crystal system**: orthorhombic
Toughness: fair	**Crystal form**: slender prisms, waterworn pebbles, fibrous masses

Absorption spectrum: weak bands at 410 nm, 441 nm, and 462 nm
Fluorescence: blue sillimanite shows weak red fluorescence under LW and SW.
Pleochroism: strong; in blue stones, colorless / light yellow / blue; otherwise may be pale
green / light green / blue; or colorless / pale brown / yellow.
Treatments: Normally none, but fracture filling is possible. Fibrous sillimanite may be dyed to
imitate more expensive stones such as ruby and emerald.
Stable to light; sensitive to heat; not attacked by acids; clean with warm soapy water.

Sillimanite was first described in 1824 for a discovery in Chester, Connecticut. It was
named after Benjamin Silliman, founder of the American Journal of Science. A common
variety of sillimanite is known as **fibrolite**, because of its fibrous nature. If the fibers are
straight and parallel, a cat's-eye effect may result when cut as a cabochon; radiating fibers
can create a star. Fibrous material may be white, gray, black, brown, yellow or grayish, green.

Sillimanite may also be clear and free of eye-visible inclusions and then is usually
faceted. The colors are typically blue, green, yellow, gray or colorless. Frequently, the tones
are light to very light. In fact, the stones are often so light that sillimanite has occasionally
been used as a diamond substitute. However, darker tones are also available.

Myanmar is noted for its fine quality blue and violet sillimanite, as well as ruby, sapphire
and jade. Sri Lanka and especially India produce much of the cat's-eye sillimanite that is
on the market, as well as other gem varieties. Other sources of sillimanite include Kenya,
Tanzania, Brazil, South Africa, Australia, Madagascar, Korea, Canada, Germany, France,
Czechoslovakia, Scotland and several states in the U.S. Most of the sillimanite found is
industrial grade and used in the manufacture of heat resistant ceramics and spark plugs.

The best quality sillimanite can retail for up to $400/ct. Low-grade stones are available
for less than $10/ct. Cat's-eye sillimanites generally retail for less than $100/ct and are
often available for less than $30/ct. Most sillimanite gems are below five carats. Larger
stones, up to 20 carats or more, are few and far between, especially in well cut stones.

In general, blue sillimanite fetches the highest prices. The more intense the color, the
higher the price. Yellow and colorless stones are also in demand; clarity, transparency and
cut can have a significant impact on their price.

Top left: Fig. Si.1 Cat's-eye sillimanite from D & J Rare Gems. *Photo by Donna Rhoads.*
Top center: Fig. Si.2 Sillimanite (5.66 ct). *Cut and photographed by Coast to Coast Rarestones.*
Top right: Fig. Si.3 Sillimanite Earrings design © by Eve J. Alfillé. *Photo by Matthew Arden.*

Smithsonite (SMITH so nite), carbonates class, calcite group
Chemical formula: $ZnCO_3$, zinc carbonate

RI: 1.621-1.850	**Cleavage**: perfect in three directions
Hardness: 4–5	**Luster**: pearly, silky, vitreous
SG: 4.3–4.45	**Optic char**: DR, uniaxial negative, aggregate
Birefringence: .225–.228	**Crystal system**: hexagonal (trigonal)
Dispersion: .037	**Pleochroism**: inert to strong, colors vary
Fracture: splintery, uneven	**Crystal shape**: massive, botryoidal aggregate
Toughness: poor	**Fluorescence**: inert to strong, colors vary
Spectrum: not diagnostic	**Treatments**: normally none except for possible fracture filling.

Stable to light, sensitive to heat, effervesces in warm acids; avoid ultrasonic cleaners.

Smithsonite is generally a translucent gem with a beautiful pearly luster, which occurs in almost every color of the spectrum and may also be multicolored. Purple and red are the most rare. Semi-transparent to transparent material is occasionally found in Tsumeb, Namibia, the premiere smithsonite source because of its wide range of colors and crystal forms. The Magdalena (Kelly) district in New Mexico is famous for its blue-green smithsonite. Other important sources of smithsonite include, Zambia, Australia, Greece, Italy, Mexico and the states of Arizona, Arkansas, and Colorado in the United States.

Smithsonite was named after English mineralogist James Smithson (1765-1829) in honor of his work differentiating between the minerals now identified as smithsonite, hemimorphite, and hydrozincite. Previously they were all called **calamine**. Smithson is better known as the benefactor who left money to establish the Smithsonian Institution in Washington, D.C.

According to mineralogist Max Bauer, in the 19th century, calamine (smithsonite) from Laurion, Greece was being worked for brooches, ring-stones, and as plates, etc. (*Precious Stones, Volume 2, p 423)*. Though seldom found in jewelry stores, smithsonite is still being carved and mounted in jewelry today. However, because of its cleavage and low hardness, it is not a good choice for rings.

Smithsonite is priced higher than other translucent to semi-transparent stones such as chrysoprase, rose quartz and prehnite. Blue smithsonites tend to cost the most because they are not common but are in high demand. According to John Bradshaw of Coast-to-Coast Rarestones International, retail values for commercial 1 carat(ish) sizes may be as little as $50/ct–$60/ct. Most good smithsonites will be priced between $100/ct–$200/ct retail. Pricing is dependent on degree of transparency, depth of color, clarity, cutting and size. On the higher end, there have been exceptional stones whose retail prices have reached $600/ct.

Two key characteristics of smithsonite are its high birefringence and high specific gravity. A good source of further information is *Smithsonite No. 13, Think Zinc!* by Lithographics, LLC.

Fig. Sm.1 Smithsonite druse earrings design © by Eve Alfillé. *Photo by Matthew Arden.*

Fig. Sm.2 Two-tone smithsonite from 79 Mine, Arizona. *Specimen & photo: The Arkenstone.*

Fig. Smi.3 American smithsonites (35.47 ct & 20.77 cts) from Pala International. *Photo by Mia Dixon.*

Fig. Smi.4 Smithsonite pendant. *Made & photographed by Carina Rossner.*

Fig. Sm.5 Cadmium smithsonite from the Shesh-donnell mine, Ireland. *Specimen and photo from Rob Lavinsky of The Arkenstone.*

Fig. Sm.6 Namibian smithsonite (23.67 cts). *Cut and photographed by Coast-to-Coast Rarestones International.*

Fig. Sm.7 Smithsonite included by hematite from Tsumeb, Nambia. *Specimen and photo from Rob Lavinsky of The Arkenstone.*

Fig. Sm.8 Cobaltian smithsonite from Choix, Sinaloa, Mexico. *Specimen and photo from Rob Lavinsky of The Arkenstone.*

Sphalerite (SFALer ite"), sulfides class, sphalerite group
Chemical formula: ZnS, zinc sulfide

RI: 2.369-2.43	**Cleavage**: perfect in six directions
Hardness: 3.5–4	**Luster**: adamantine to subadamantine
SG: 3.90–4.10	**Optic char**: SR
Birefringence: none	**Fracture**: conchoidal to uneven
Dispersion: .156	**Pleochroism**: none
Crystal system: cubic	**Crystal shape**: dodecahedral, tetrahedral, massive
Toughness: poor	**Spectrum**: 651, 667, 690 nm lines

Fluorescence: usually inert, but sometimes moderate to strong orange-red to LW and SW; Material from Otavi, Namibia is triboluminescent, meaning light is generated when the material is scratched, rubbed or crushed. **Treatments**: Normally none; possible fracture filling
Stable to light; sensitive to heat; attacked by hydrochloric acid; avoid ultrasonic cleaners.

Sphalerite is a lively, brilliant gem that is usually yellow, orange or red and has three times the fire of a diamond. Gem-grade material is also occasionally green or bicolored, showing, for example, both yellow and orange face-up. A chief ore of zinc, most sphalerite is industrial quality, and translucent to opaque with a dark brown or black color due to iron in its chemical makeup. Unfortunately, it is very fragile because of its low hardness (3.5–4) and six directions of perfect cleavage. Therefore, don't wear sphalerite in a ring; instead, display its beauty in a pendant or earrings.

Fig. Spha.1 Bulgarian sphalerite. *Courtesy the Arkenstone.*

Santander, Spain has been the most important source of red, orange and yellow sphalerite, but it is no longer being mined there because that locale is now a national park. Other sources include China, Bulgaria, Italy, Morocco, Peru, Australia, and the United States.

Most transparent faceted sphalerite below five carats retails for between $20ct– $150/ct. Large stones with exceptional clarity, color intensity, and cut quality can retail for as much as $400/ct, and if green, $600/ct. Sphalerites above 20 carats are available.

Figs. Spha.2–4 Spanish sphalerites from Pala International. *Photos by Mia Dixon.*

Fig. Spha.5 Sphalerite cabs from Iteco Inc. *Photo © Renée Newman.*

Fig. Spha.6 Chinese sphalerite. *Crystals and photo from The Arkenstone.*

Taaffeite (TAR fite), oxides class. As of 2002, the International Mineralogical Association-approved mineral name is **magnesiotaaffeite-2N'2S**.
Chemical formula: $BeMg_3Al_8O_{16}$, beryllium magnesium aluminum oxide

RI: 1.718–1.724	**Luster**: vitreous
Hardness: 8–8.5	**Pleochroism**: weak
SG: 3.60–3.62	**Optic char**: DR, uniaxial negative
Birefringence: .004–.005	**Fluorescence**: inert to weak green (LW and SW)
Dispersion: .019	**Fracture**: conchoidal, uneven
Crystal system: hexagonal	**Crystal form**: prismatic, grains, waterworn pebbles
Toughness: good	**Absorption spectrum**: weak band at 458 nm, not diagnostic
Cleavage: none	**Treatments**: normally none, fracture filling possible

Stable to light; reaction to heat undetermined; not attacked by chemicals.

Taaffeite is a rare purple, violet, pink or colorless transparent gem, which was named after Count Taaffe, a Dublin gemologist who discovered the first taaffeite in a jeweler's junk box in 1945. It resembled a mauve spinel, a gem with a similar hardness, density and refractive index, but unlike spinel, the unknown stone was doubly refractive. Curiosity prompted Taaffe to send it to the Precious Stone Laboratory in London for identification. After conducting a chemical and x-ray analysis of the stone, the lab determined it was a new mineral. This was the first time a new mineral was discovered as a faceted stone rather than as gem rough.

Fig. Taff.1 Sri Lankan taaffeite (8.50 ct) from Pala International. *Photo by Wimon Manorotkul.*

The primary source of taaffeite is Sri Lanka, where it is found as pebbles in river beds and lake sediments. In recent years, some taaffeites have come from Tunduru, Tanzania and Mogok, Myanmar. Because of its hardness and lack of cleavage, taaffeite is a suitable ring stone. It is also a prestigious gem for mineral collectors. High demand in addition to its rarity, durability and beauty make it one of the most expensive rare gems. Retail prices for stones between 1–2 carats can range roughly from $1000/ct–$3500/ct. Taaffeites above 2 carats may retail for as much as $8,000/ct depending on size, color intensity, clarity and cut quality. In general, stones cut for maximum brilliance and color coverage sell for significantly more per carat than stones cut to maximize weight.

Fig. Taff.2 Taaffeites from Pala International. *Photo by Mia Dixon.*

Fig. Taff.3 A rare complete hexagonal taaffeite crystal (1.3 x 1.3 x .6 cm) from Sri Lanka. *Crystal and photo from Rob Lavinsky of The Arkenstone.*

Tugtupite (TUG tuh pite), member of the sodalite group and silicates class
Chemical formula: $Na_4AlBeSi_4O_{12}Cl$, sodium aluminum beryllium silicate chloride

RI: 1.496–1.502   **Cleavage**: distinct
Hardness: 4–6.5   **Toughness**: fair to good
SG: 2.33–2.57   **Optic char**: DR, uniaxial positive, aggregate
Birefringence: .006–.008   **Fracture**: conchoidal to uneven
Luster: vitreous   **Pleochroism**: moderate purplish red & orange-red, none in aggregate
Crystal system: tetragonal   **Crystal shape**: usually massive, short tetragonal prisms
Fluorescence: red areas—moderate to strong orange (LW), orangish red (SW), may phosphoresce,
     darkens when exposed to UV or sunlight, but returns to lighter tone when placed in the dark
Avoid heat, chemicals and ultrasonic cleaners; wash with warm soapy water.

     Discovered around 1960 at Tugtup in Greenland, tugtupite is usually pink to red and mottled with white, gray or black. When the stone is placed in sunlight, pale colors deepen and when placed in the dark, the color fades back to a lighter hue. This is a property called **tenebrescence**. Tugtupite also has a distinctive fluorescence under ultraviolet light. Though found in Russia and Quebec, Canada, tugtupites from Greenland are the only commercially available stones. Most of the material is non-crystalline and translucent to semi-opaque, and is either carved or cut as moderately priced cabochons; transparent faceted stones are very rare. According to John Bradshaw of Coast-to-Coast Rarestones, pricing for the Greenland material can run from $20/ct-$100/ct retail for cabochons. Depending on degree of size, transparency, clarity, cutting, etc., faceted stones can retail between $200/ct-$2000/ct.

Figs. Tug.1 & Tug.2 Tugtupites from Narsaq Greenland. *Gems and photos from Coast-to-Coast Rarestones International.*

Fig. Tug.3 Tugtupite pendant after exposure to UV light. The rough on the right is from the same material as the pendant, but it has not been exposed to UV light. The rough will turn the same color as the pendant if it is also exposed because tugtupite is tenebrescent. The material also glows in the dark after exposure to UV. *Pendant & photo by Mark Anderson of Different Seasons Jewelry.*

Variscite (VAIR is site) a member of the variscite group and phosphates class
Chemical formula: $AlPO_4.2H_2O$, hydrous aluminum phosphate

RI: 1.560–1.590, spot 1.57
Hardness: 3.5–5
SG: 2.40–2.60
Birefringence: .031
Pleochroism: none
Toughness: poor
Magnetism: inert to moderate

Cleavage: good in one direction, but rarely visible.
Luster: waxy to vitreous
Optic char: DR, aggregate
Fracture: granular, uneven, splintery, octahedral (rare)
Crystal system: orthorhombic
Crystal form: massive, nodules, crusts
Fluorescence: inert to weak green (LW and SW)

Absorption spectrum: strong line at 688 nm, weaker line at 650 nm
Treatments: frequently impregnated with plastic to improve durability and polish; often dyed to improve color.   Stable to light; sensitive to heat, attacked by acids; avoid ultrasonics.

Variscite is usually semi-opaque and yellow-green to blue-green, but it can be pink and translucent to transparent. Named after Variscia, the old name of the German district of Voightland, where it was first discovered, variscite is often mistaken for turquoise. Brazil, Queensland in Australia, and Utah and Nevada in the US are four other important sources.

Variscite from Utah is often veined or mottled with minerals such as yellow crandallite, brown hydroxlapatite, and dark green wardite, which provide designers with interesting patterns for creative jewelry. Material from Nevada may have a dark spider-web-like veining and has erroneously been called Nevada turquoise. Pink variscite has been found in Ghana and Brazil; some of it is identified as ferroan variscite. Crystallized green variscite has also been found in Brazil, but is rare and usually only sold as mineral specimens.

Green semi-opaque variscite is a popular stone for carvings, bowls, spheres, pendants and Indian jewelry. Its pricing is similar to that of turquoise.

Fig. Va.1 Variscite from Fairfield, Utah with crandallite, montgomeryite, and wardite. *Specimen and photo from Rob Lavinsky of The Arkenstone.*

Fig. Va.2 Variscite jewelry by Tom DeGasperis of Dancing Designs. *Photo by Shelly Smith.*

Fig. Va.3 Magenta ferroan variscite from Minas Gerais, Brazil. *The Arkenstone.*

How to Care for Rare & Unusual Gems

Which of the following gems is hardest? Which is most durable?

1. Amber
2. Pearl
3. Malachite
4. Turquoise

According to the *GIA Gem Reference Guide*, turquoise is the hardest, but pearls could be considered the most durable, particularly if they have thick nacre or no bead nucleus. Here's what the GIA Gemological Institute of America has to say about the above gems:

1. **Amber**—hardness: 2–2.5; toughness: poor; fine crazing often develops with age; attacked by acids and strong solvents
3. **Malachite**—hardness: 3.5–4; toughness: poor; attacked by acids
2. **Pearl**—hardness: 2.5–4; toughness: usually good, but variable; outer surface may be scratched or fractured very easily; affected by age, dehydration, or excessive bleaching; attacked by all acids and often by perspiration or perfume.
4. **Turquoise**—hardness: 5–6; fine quality is fair to good; chalky untreated material is poor and fractures easily; may be discolored by perspiration and cosmetics.

As you can see, amber, malachite, pearls and turquoise are fragile gems. They're not very hard and they are easily affected by chemicals. Yet for centuries, they have been used as popular jewelry materials because people learned how to care for them.

Many of the gems in this book have been considered by others to be unsuitable for jewelry and only of use to collectors. One of the ideas I hope you'll take away from this book is that all of the gems in it can be used in jewelry even though special setting techniques and secure bezels may be required to protect them. The jewelry images in this guide provide ideas on how this can be accomplished. Treatments can also make some gems more practical for jewelry wear. For example, durability may sometimes be increased by impregnating porous stones with an epoxy or plastic substance, a process called stabilization.

One jeweler explained that he would never sell a kyanite because it would scratch too easily when placed in a jewelry box. (Kyanite, by the way, has a variable hardness of 4–5 in one direction and 6–7.5 in another, which is harder than some traditional gemstones). It is true that kyanite can get scratched, but so can gold, silver and most gemstones sold in jewelry stores, particularly if they are jumbled together with diamond jewelry.

Look at the fluorite necklace in figure 3.1. Appraiser and jewelry designer Jane Ramsey has worn it every couple of weeks for more than five years and it still looks fine. Fluorite has a hardness of 4 and perfect cleavage in four directions. According to many trade members, these physical characteristics would render fluorite too fragile for jewelry use. However, the designer hangs the necklace separately on a hook in a jewelry armoire, where it

Fig. 3.1 Fluorite jewelry designed by Jane Ramsey and worn regularly for more than five years. *Photo © Renée Newman.*

doesn't come in contact with other jewelry. If she had thrown it on a dresser or jumbled it in a box, the necklace would be scratched and dull-looking.

Storing Your Jewelry

There are a variety of ways to protect jewelry from damage during storage:

1. **Cloth-lined jewelry boxes with partitions and slots** to keep jewelry separated. Avoid placing these on tables or dressers where burglars can easily spot them.

2. **Stackable jewelry trays with partitions** (fig. 3.2).

Fig. 3.2 Stackable jewelry tray with well-protected mother-of-pearl antique Chinese gambling counters from Timeless Gems. *Photo © Renée Newman.*

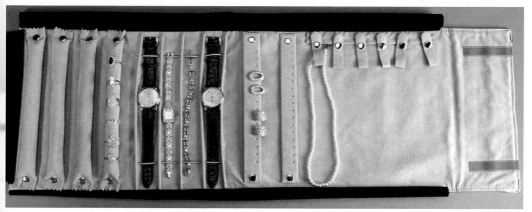

Fig. 3.3 Jewelry roll made of Italian suede. *Roll and photo courtesy of A & A Jewelry Supply.*

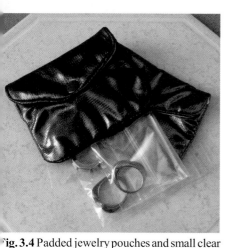

Fig. 3.4 Padded jewelry pouches and small clear plastic pouches. *Photo © Renée Newman.*

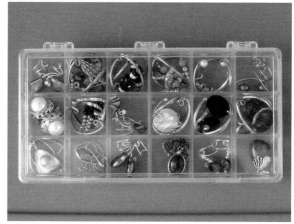

Fig. 3.5 Partitioned clear plastic box allowing easy jewelry viewing. *Photo © Renée Newman.*

3. **Jewelry rolls** that open up with a large display area for viewing jewelry (fig 3.3)

4. **Padded jewelry pouches** (fig 3.4) **or padded bags with lots of pockets.** A disadvantage of this method is that you can't see your jewelry and find it readily.

5. **Small clear plastic pouches and bags** for storing pieces separately (fig. 3.4). These are inexpensive and allow you to view your jewelry quickly. The individual plastic pouches can then be organized in ordinary boxes or in a safe.

6. **Clear plastic boxes with partitions** (fig. 3.5) These, too, have the advantage of allowing the jewelry to be viewed easily. The boxes can be covered with a cloth or bag so the jewelry is not obvious when stored in a drawer or cupboard.

Needless to say, the safest place for storing expensive jewelry or gems is in a safe or bank vault. Make sure, however, that jewelry pieces and gemstones are separated from each other.

Which Gemstones Are the Most Durable?

Gemstone durability involves several factors:

1. **Resistance to scratching**. The harder a gemstone is, the more resistant it is to scratching. You can find the Mohs hardness of the gems in this book in their individual data tables and in the appendix, which lists all the stones in this book as well as those in the *Gemstone Buying Guide* by their descending hardness.

2. **Resistance to fracture, cleavage and chipping**. This is determined by the cleavage, density, hardness, and internal structure of the gemstone. It is possible for stones to have perfect cleavage and still be very durable. For example, diamond has perfect cleavage in four directions, but it is one of the most durable gems available. That's because of its internal structure, superior hardness and resistance to heat and chemicals. It takes great skill and force to cleave a diamond. However, in most other cases, stones with perfect cleavage are more susceptible to damage than stones with no cleavage or poor cleavage. A low hardness and density can also have a negative impact on fracture resistance. Aggregates such as banded rhodochrosite are generally more fracture resistant than their transparent crystalline counterparts. Any gemstone with large fractures has reduced durability.

3. **Resistance to damage from heat**. Gems have various reactions to high heat. Hematite becomes magnetic; aragonite converts to calcite; danburite fuses (melts) under a jeweler's torch, sodalite fuses to a colorless glass; opal loses water and crazes; rhodochrosite darkens and breaks into pieces under a jeweler's torch; any stone with liquid inclusions can fracture as the inclusions expand with heat. In addition, fractures already present in stones can expand. It is therefore best to keep gems away from heat if you don't know how they will react to it and avoid sudden changes of temperatures. You should not, for example, lie in the sun and then jump in a swimming pool while wearing these gems, nor should you go from a hot oven to a cold sink of water or from a hot tub to a cold shower. If you do, the sudden change of temperature could possibly cause the stones to crack or shatter. When available, heat sensitivity information has been included it in the gem descriptions.

4. **Resistance to damage from chemicals**. Many gems are attacked by acids and other chemicals. Some of these stones include ammolite, calcite, brazilianite, prehnite, scapolite, scheelite, serpentine, sphene, and variscite. Do not clean these gems with harsh chemicals or bring them into contact with acidic substances such as lemon juice and vinegar.

5. **Resistance to damage from long exposure to strong light**. Some stones such as chrysocolla, pink apatite, irradiated fluorite, and larimar may fade upon prolonged exposure to strong sunlight. Don't leave these gems sitting on a sunny window sill or place them in a display window. The light can make them fade and the heat can cause small cracks to appear. The data tables of the gem descriptions indicate if the stones are stable to light or not. In a few cases, light stability information was not included because it was not available.

Curiously, some stones such as tugtupite darken in sunlight, but when placed in the dark, the color fades back to a lighter hue, a property called tenebrescence.

The most durable gems in this book are taaffeite, phenakite, dumortierite, danburite, and jeremejevite. They all have a Mohs hardness of at least 7, and none of the gems has perfect cleavage. Red beryl has a hardness of 7.5–8, but it typically has a low clarity and requires fracture filling. As a result, most red beryl is not as resistant to fractures as for example, a danburite, which has a hardness of 7–7.5.

Other unusually durable gemstones include diamond, alexandrite, chrysoberyl, spinel, and ruby or sapphire that has not been fracture filled. They can be cleaned with ultrasonic and steam cleaners. Lead glass-filled rubies (composite rubies), however, are not durable. Household cleaners and lemon juice can turn the filler white and a jeweler's torch can melt the filler causing the stone to break into pieces.

Choosing a Setting for Fragile Gemstones

Bezel settings and wire wrapping are the safest settings for fragile gemstones. A bezel is a band of metal that surrounds a gem and holds it in place. In the past, bezel settings were used primarily for cabochons (unfaceted, dome-shaped stones) such as jade. They have become popular now as attractive settings for faceted stones, too. The bezel may either fully or partially encircle the stone (figs. 3.6 –3.8). A bezel setting offers several advantages: it provides good protection for the girdle and pavilion areas of gems; it can be used to set almost all gemstones without causing damage to them; it accentuates the circumference of the stone, making it appear larger than in a prong setting; and it provides a smooth ring surface that does not snag clothing.

Sometimes metal is simply wrapped around the stone as shown in figures 3.6 & 3.9 or partially wrapped and secured with prongs as in figure 3.10.

Wire wrapping is a convenient way of setting freeforms and crystals (3.11 & 12).

Fig. 3.6 Cobaltocalcite druse bezel-set and wrapped in silver in jewelry by Carina Rossner. *Photo by George Post.*

Fig. 3.7 Sphene ring with bezel setting. *Ring and photo by Timeless Gems.*

Fig. 3.8 Diamond ring with partial bezel setting. *Ring and photo by Varna.*

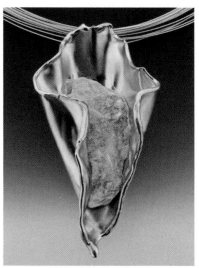

Fig. 3.9 Lepidolite wrapped in silver in a calla lily pendant by Carina Rossner. *Photo by George Post.*

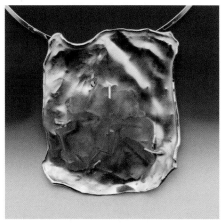

Fig. 3.10 Fluorite secured by prongs and protected by metal in a pendant by Carina Rossner. *Photo by George Post.*

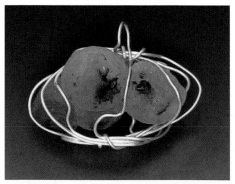

Fig. 3.11 Wire-wrapped prehnite with epidote inclusions. *Pendant & photo by Carina Rossner.*

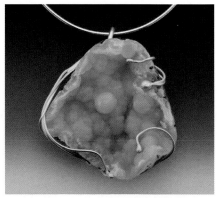

Fig. 3.12 Wire-wrapped hemimorphite pendant by Carina Rossner. *Photo: George Post.*

How to Clean Fragile Gemstones

If all gems were like diamonds, it would be easy to clean them. Untreated diamonds without bad fractures can be steam cleaned, boiled in acid, soaked in alcohol or vigorously vibrated in ultrasonic cleaners. These cleaning methods would ruin many other gems.

The safest way to clean a gemstone and its mounting is to regularly wipe it lightly with a soft cloth moistened with warm soapy water, provided that the stone has a smooth surface and is not druse (an incrustation of small crystals on the surface of a rock or mineral). Then dry it with a soft, lint-free cloth. Gems that are not damaged by ammonia (i.e., andalusite, phenakite, diamonds, etc.) can be cleaned by spraying them with a window cleaner. However, do not spray fragile stones or gems that are damaged by chemicals. If the dirt can't be washed off with a cloth, try using a toothpick or a pressurized stream of water from a Waterpik or shower head to remove it.

Carina Rossner, who specializes in jewelry with fragile and rare minerals, advises her clients to clean dirt and oils off her pieces with an old toothbrush and dishwashing soap. If that doesn't work, have the piece professionally cleaned. Jewelers often clean stones with ultrasonic cleaners, which send high frequency sound waves through solutions. The vibrating fluid removes built-up dirt, but it can also shake poorly-set stones from their mountings and damage some types of gems.

Chapter 12 of the *Gemstone Buying Guide* has a table, which summarizes cleaning precautions required for the major gems. The gem descriptions in *Rare Gemstones* include warnings about ultrasonic cleaning. In general, it is best not to use ultrasonics for the majority of the gems in this book.

Miscellaneous Tips

♦ If possible, avoid wearing jewelry while participating in contact sports or doing housework, gardening, repairs, etc. The mounting can be damaged, and stones can be chipped, scratched and cracked. During rough work, if you want to wear a ring for sentimental reasons or to avoid losing it, wear protective gloves. Hopefully, your ring has a smooth setting style with no high prongs.

♦ When you place jewelry near a sink, make sure the drains are plugged or that it is put in a protective container. Otherwise, don't take the jewelry off.

♦ Clean your jewelry on a regular basis. Then you won't have to use risky procedures to clean it later on.

♦ When making any repair or alteration to jewelry with fragile minerals, remove the stone first and the reset it after the change has been completed.

♦ Don't remove rings by pulling on any of their gemstones. Instead, grasp the metal ring portion. This will help prevent the stones from coming loose and getting dirty.

♦ Occasionally, check your jewelry for loose stones. Shake it or tap it lightly with your forefinger while holding it next to your ear. If you hear the stones rattle or click, have a jeweler tighten the prongs.

◆ Take a photo of your jewelry (a macro lens is helpful). Simply lay it all together on a table for the photo. If the jewelry is ever lost or stolen, you'll have documentation to help you remember and prove what you had. Expensive jewelry should be documented and appraised by a professional jewelry appraiser. My website **www.reneenewman.com** has a list of independent jewelry appraisers and appraisal organization links.

◆ About every six months, have a jewelry professional check your ring for loose stones or wear on the mounting. Many jewelers will do this free of charge, and they'll be happy to answer your questions regarding the care of your jewelry.

Where to Find an Appraiser

Several people have asked me for recommendations for jewelry and gem appraisers, so I created a list of independent appraisers who are gemologists and who have completed formal education in appraisal procedures, ethics and law. You can find it on my website www.reneenewman.com by clicking on the "appraisers" link, or you can go directly to the appraisers' page at www.reneenewman.com/appraisers.htm. Because I haven't met all of these appraisers, this list is not an endorsement; it's just for your convenience.

There are also highly qualified appraisers who work in jewelry stores. You can locate them and independent appraisers as well by contacting the following organizations:

American Gem Society (AGS)
8881 W. Sahara Ave, Las Vegas, NV 89117
Phone (866) 805-6500, www.americangemsociety.org/find-an-appraiser

American Society of Appraisers (ASA)
555 Herndon Parkway, Suite 125, Herndon, VA 20170
Phone (703) 478-2228, Fax (703) 742-8471, www.appraisers.org

The Association of Independent Jewellery Valuers (AIJV)
Algo Business Centre, Glenearn Road, Perth, Scotland PH2 ONJ, United Kingdom
Phone +44 (0) 1738 450477, e-mail: info@aijv.org, www.aijv.org

Canadian Jeweller's Institute
27 Queen St. East, Suite 600, Toronto, Ontario M5C 2M6 Canada
Phone (416) 368-7616 ext 223, Fax (416) 368-1986
www.canadianjewellers.com/html/aapmemberlist.htm

International Society of Appraisers (ISA)
303 West Madison Street, Suite 2650, Chicago, IL 60606
Phone (312) 981-6778, Fax (312) 265-2908, www.isa-appraisers.org

National Association of Jewelry Appraisers (NAJA)
P.O. Box 18, Rego Park, New York, 11374-0018
Phone (718) 896-1536, www.NAJAappraisers.com

Value the Past (An appraisal service that specializes in antique and estate jewelry and personal property)
Phone (877) 797-9011, Fax (866) 551-5017, www.valuethepast.com

In Australia, you can find appraisers through the following branches of the National Council of Jewelry Valuers:

National Council of Jewellery Valuers, Inc. (NCJV)
Level 2 Suite 213, 155 King Street, Sydney, NSW 2000, Australia
Phone 02 9232 6599, Fax 02 9232 6399, www.ncjv.com.au

NCJV Inc. (Queensland)
Grange, Queensland, Australia
Phone/Fax 07 3857 4377 Email: qld@ncjv.com.au

NCJV Inc. (South Australia Division)
Henley Beach, South Australia, Australia
Phone 08 8234 2505, Fax 08 8125 5822 Email: sa@ncjv.com.au

NCJV Inc. (Tasmania Division)
Hobart, Tasmania, Australia
Phone 03 6234 2426, Fax 03 6231 5366 Email: tas@ncjv.com.au

NCJV Inc., (Victoria Division)
Melbourne, VIC Australia
Phone 03 9500 9250, Fax 03 9500 2904 Email: vic@ncjv.com.au

NCJV Inc., Western Australia, Australia
Perth, WA Australia
Phone 08 9409 2009, Fax 08 9364 5504 Email: wa@ncjv.com.au

After you get the names of some appraisers, you'll need to interview them to find out if they are qualified to appraise your jewelry. When interviewing an appraiser you should ask:

◆ What are your qualifications? Basic information about gemological and appraisal credentials is provided on my website at reneenewman.com/qa.htm.

◆ How much do you charge?

◆ What does your appraisal fee include? The last chapter of *Volume 1* of *Exotic Gems* outlines what a good appraisal includes. More detailed appraisal information is also available in my *Gem & Jewelry Pocket Guide* and *Ruby, Sapphire & Emerald Buying Guide.*

◆ What experience do you have in valuing the items requiring an appraisal? For example, if you have period jewelry (Art Deco, Art Nouveau, Victorian, etc.), the appraiser should know the market for it in order for you to obtain an accurate value. The same is true for colored stones. It's fairly straightforward to appraise contemporary jewelry with diamonds, but rare colored gems and other types of jewelry may require specialized experience.

A good interview can provide information you'll need to select an experienced and ethical appraiser who provides thorough and accurate appraisals.

Appendix

Main Sources of Information for the Identification Data

The bibliography provides a complete list of the written sources of information for this book, but some were used more often than others, especially for the data in the identification tables. These include:

Color Encyclopedia of Gemstones by Joel Arem
Dana's Manual of Mineralogy
Gem-A Diploma in Gemmology Course
Gems by Robert Webster\
Gems & Lapidary Materials by June Culp Zeitner
Gemstone and Mineral Data Book by John Sinkankas
Gemstones by Karen Hurell and Mary L. Johnson
The Gemstones Handbook by Arthur Thomas
GIA Gem Identification Lab Manual
GIA Gem Reference Guide
Handbook of Gem Identification by Richard T. Liddicoat
Rock Forming Minerals by Deer, Howie & Zussman
Rocks & Minerals by Frederick H. Pough
www.gemologyonline.com
www.mindat.org
www.webmineral.com

The magnetism information was based primarily on the "Magnetic Susceptibility Index for Gemstones" chart © 2010 by Kirk Feral and http://gemstonemagnetism.com. Some magnetism information is from www.webmineral.com. Don Hoover, an expert on gem magnetism, was another source. He says that all substances containing atoms are magnetic in the sense that all are affected by a magnetic field, either repelled (diamagnetic) or attracted (paramagnetic). For example, pure corundum is diamagnetic, however most of the gem corundum are colored, and the coloring agents may make them attracted to a magnet. Thus, most minerals and gems can range from diamagnetic to paramagnetic. Most colorless minerals, however, will be diamagnetic.

Birthstones established in 1912 by the American National Retail Jewelers' Assn:

Month	Stone	Month	Stone
January	Garnet	July	Ruby
February	Amethyst	August	Peridot or sardonyx
March	Aquamarine or bloodstone	September	Sapphire
April	Diamond	October	Opal or tourmaline
May	Emerald	November	Topaz
June	Pearl or moonstone	December	Turquoise or lapis lazuli

Gemstone Identification Terms Explained

Gemstones may be identified as a group, species or variety. A **group** is composed of a number of closely related species. "Sodalite" is an example of a group name and a species name. A **species** name refers to a mineral with a characteristic crystal structure and chemical composition. Tugtupite, sodalite and haüyne are species and members of the sodalite group. A **variety** name is normally based on color, transparency or optical effects such as iridescence and cat's-eye patterns. For example, hackmanite is a pink or lavender variety of sodalite that can fade to colorless or white. It has the same essential chemistry and crystal structure as sodalite but differs in color and usually in transparency. Each gem species has characteristics which distinguish it from other species. For easy reference, we'll list some of these characteristics below with their definitions.

Refractive Index (RI): the degree to which light is bent as it passes through the stone. This is measured with an instrument called a refractometer. Most colored gems have RI's that range between 1.43 and 2.00. Diamonds have an RI of approximately 2.42, which means they bend light about 2.42 times more than air does. This also means that light travels 2.42 times more slowly through diamonds than it does through air. As a general rule, the higher the RI is, the greater the potential brilliance of the stone. Other factors such as clarity, cut and color also affect brilliance. There can be some variation in the RI of a species depending on a stone's origin and color. This is because of the presence of impurities, which can vary according to the source of the stone. Thus the RI of a species may fall slightly above or below the RI ranges listed in this book.

Specific Gravity (SG): a ratio comparing the weight of a gem to the weight of an equal volume of water at 4 °C. The greater the density, the higher the SG. The SG of most colored gemstones falls between 2.00 and 5.00.

Hardness: the resistance of a gem to scratching and abrasion. This can be classified using the Mohs scale of hardness. The Mohs scale rates the relative hardness of materials with numbers from 1 to 10. The 10 rating of a diamond is the highest and the 1 of talc is the lowest. The intervals between numbers on the scale are not equal, especially between 9 and 10. Ruby and sapphire rate a 9, but a diamond may be more than 100 times harder. Some gems like diamond even have a directional hardness where one direction or surface is harder than another.

Toughness: the resistance of a gem to breaking, chipping or cracking. This is different from hardness. Jade is a relatively soft gem (6–7), yet it is the toughest.

Cleavage: the tendency for a mineral to split along crystal planes, where the atomic bonding is weak. A gemstone may have one or more directions of cleavage, which are classified as perfect (almost perfectly smooth), distinct or indistinct. Cleavage has a negative impact on toughness. Directions of weakness that are not true cleavages are called **parting**.

Crystal System: one of the seven classifications of the internal structure of a crystal. It is based on the symmetry of the crystal structure. The simplest and most symmetrical system is called isometric or cubic. The other six systems in the order of their decreasing symmetry are tetragonal, hexagonal, trigonal, orthorhombic, monoclinic and triclinic.

For descriptions and diagrams of the seven crystal systems, consult: www.webmineral.com/crystall.shtml. Materials that don't have a crystalline structure (e.g., glass) are called **amorphous.** Some gems such as jade and agate are composed of minute crystals intricately grown together. These gems are technically classified as aggregates (AGG) and are usually translucent to opaque.

Optic Character: the effect a gem material has on light. If it can split light into two rays, each traveling at different speeds, then it is **doubly refractive (DR).** If it does not split light, the stone is **singly refractive (SR)**. In a doubly refractive gem, there is either one or two directions in which light is not split as it passes through it. In other words, a DR stone will behave as if it is singly refractive in at least one direction. The directions of single refraction are called **optic axes**. If the stone has one direction of single refraction, it is **uniaxial,** if it has two, it is **biaxial**.

Doubly refractive gems will have two RI's if they are uniaxial and three RI's if they are biaxial. The numerical difference between the highest and lowest RI is called the **birefringence** or **birefraction**. When you look through stones with a high birefrin-gence, such as rhodochrosite, the inclusions and facet edges will appear to be doubled.

Besides indicating if a gem is biaxial or uniaxial, this book also gives the optic sign (+ or –). If a uniaxial gem is positive, the lower RI is constant and the higher variable. A negative sign would indicate the reverse. If a biaxial gem is positive, the intermediate RI is closer to the low RI. If negative, it's closer to the high RI.

Fluorescence: the glow or emission of light by a material when it's stimulated by ultraviolet light, x-rays or other forms of radiation. The term "fluorescence" comes from the mineral fluorite (calcium fluoride), which is noted for displaying an array of intense fluorescent colors. The presence or lack of fluorescence and its color and strength can be helpful in identifying gems. **LW** stands for long-wave ultraviolet (UV) light. **SW** refers to shortwave UV radiation.

Pleochroism: the ability of certain gem materials to exhibit different colors when viewed from different directions under transmitted light. A tanzanite, for example, may appear blue in one direction, purple in another and greenish yellow in a third direction. Since it can show three colors, it is **trichroic**. Stones like sapphire, which can display two colors, are **dichroic**. The strength of pleochroism can range from very weak to very strong. In pastel and colorless stones, pleochroism may not be visible.

Dispersion: the separation of white light into spectral colors. "Dispersion" also refers to the numerical difference in the refractive indices of a red ray and violet ray passing through a gem material. The dispersion value of diamond is always 0.044. However, the amount of dispersion (fire) that a diamond displays varies depending on how it's cut and the lighting under which it is viewed.

Absorption Spectrum: the dark lines or bands that are superimposed on a spectrum of red, orange, yellow, green blue and violet. The lines indicate the presence of certain chemical elements in a gem by showing which wavelengths are absorbed. The spectrum can be viewed through an instrument called a spectroscope, which examines light that has traversed or been reflected from the specimen. Many gems have characteristic spectra.

Gemstones in the Order of their Descending Mohs Hardness

Gemstone	Hardness	Gemstone	Hardness	Gemstone	Hardness
Diamond	10	Vesuvianite	6.5	Fluorite	4
Ruby	9	Sillimanite	6–7.5	Rhodochrosite	4
Sapphire	9	Epidote	6–7	Magnesite	3.5–4.5
Alexandrite	8.5	Tanzanite	6–7	Aragonite	3.5–4
Chrysoberyl	8.5	Unakite	6–7	Azurite	3.5–4
Taaffeite	8–8.5	Zoisite	6–7	Cuprite	3.5–4
Spinel	8	Amazonite	6–6.5	Malachite	3.5–4
Topaz	8	Andesine	6–6.5	Phosphosiderite	3.5–4
Aquamarine	7.5–8	Benitoite	6–6.5	Sphalerite	3.5–4
Beryl	7.5–8	Labradorite	6–6.5	Coral	3–4
Bixbite	7.5–8	Marcasite	6–6.5	Howlite	3–3.5
Phenakite	7.5–8	Moonstone	6–6.5	Calcite	3
Emerald	7.5–8	Nephrite	6–6.5	Serpentine	2.5–5.5
Dumortierite	7–8.5	Prehnite	6–6.5	Pearl	2.5–4.5
Almandine	7–7.5	Pyrite	6–6.5	Lepidolite	2.5–4
Danburite	7–7.5	Amblygonite	6	Gold	2.5–3
Pyrope	7–7.5	Maw-sit-sit	6	Silver	2.5–3
Rhodolite	7–7.5	Orthoclase	6	Chrysocolla	2–4
Spessartine	7–7.5	Sugilite	5.5–6.5	Amber	2–2.5
Tourmaline	7–7.5	Hematite	5.5–6.5	Seraphinite	2–2.5
Uvarovite	7–7.5	Opal	5.5–6.5		
Amethyst	7	Rhodonite	5.5–6.5		
Ametrine	7	Actinolite	5.5–6		
Citrine	7	Haüyne	5.5–6		
Jeremejevite	7	Scapolite	5.5–6		
Rose Quartz	7	Sodalite	5.5–6		
Smoky Quartz	7	Tugtupite	5.5–6		
Tiger's-eye	7	Bronzite	5.5		
Andalusite	6.5–7.5	Enstatite	5.5		
Grossular	6.5–7.5	Moldavite	5.5		
Spessartine	6.5–7.5	Charoite	5–6		
Tsavorite	6.5–7.5	Diopside	5–6		
Andradite	6.5–7	Hypersthene	5–6		
Chalcedony	6.5–7	Lapis lazuli	5–6		
Demantoid	6.5–7	Psilomelane	5–6		
Zircon	6–7.5	Turquoise	5–6		
Agate	6.5–7	Brazilianite	5–5.5		
Axinite	6.5–7	Obsidian	5–5.5		
Diaspore	6.5–7	Sphene (titanite)	5–5.5		
Hiddenite	6.5–7	Apatite	5		
Jadeite	6.5–7	Hemimorphite	5		
Jasper	6.5–7	Smithsonite	5		
Kornerupine	6.5–7	Gaspéite	4.5–5		
Kunzite	6.5–7	Larimar	4.5–5		
Peridot	6.5–7	Scheelite	4.5–5		
Sinhalite	6.5–7	Kyanite	4–7.5		
Spodumene	6.5–7	Variscite	4–5		
Tiger's eye	6.5–7	Platinum	4–4.5		
Zultanite	6.5–7	Ammolite	4		

Gemstones in the Order of their Descending Refractive Index

Hematite	2.94–3.22	Andalusite	1.63–1.65	Haüyne	1.494–1.505
Cuprite	2.848–2.850	Danburite	1.630–1.636	Calcite	1.486–1.658
Diamond	2.417–2.419	Smithsonite	1.621–1.850	Moldavite	1.48–1.51
Sphalerite	2.369–2.43	Prehnite	1.616–1.649	Obsidian	1.48–1.5
Scheelite	1.918.–1.937	Tourmaline	1.614–1.666	Sodalite	1.48
Sphene	1.88–2.05	Hemimorphite	1.614–1.636	Hackmanite	1.48
Demantoid	1.841–1.887	Gaspéite	1.61–1.83	Chrysocolla	1.460–1.570
Melanite	1.88–1.94	Turquoise	1.610–1.650	Glass	1.44–1.90
Uvarovite	1.798–1.864	Topaz	1.609–1.643	Fluorite	1.43–1.44
YAG	1.833	Sugilite	1.602–1.611	Opal	1.37–1.52
Zircon	1.810–2.024	Brazilianite	1.60–1.623		
Spessartine	1.774–1.814	Nephrite	1.600–1.627		
Almandine	1.78–1.830	Larimar	1.59–1.64		
Mali garnet	1.762–1.841	Howlite	1.583–1.608		
Ruby	1.762–1.778	Rhodochrosite	1.578–1.840		
Sapphire	1.762–1.778	Amblygonite	1.578–1.646		
Benitoite	1.757–1.804	Seraphinite	1.571–1.599		
Malaya garnet	1.75–1.78	Emerald	1.57–1.60		
Rhodolite	1.75–1.795	Aquamarine	1.567–1.590		
Chrysoberyl	1.746-1.763	Red beryl	1.564–1.574		
Alexandrite	1.746–1..763	Variscite	1.56–1.59		
Grossular	1.73–1.770	Serpentine	1.551–1.574		
Hessonite	1.73–1.75	Labradorite	1.559–1.572		
Epidote	1,729–1.768	Charoite	1.548–1.561		
Azurite	1.730 1.846	Amethyst	1.544–1.553		
Pyrope	1.714–1.75	Citrine,	1.544–1.553		
Taaffeite	1.718–1.724	Rock crystal	1.544–1.553		
Rhodonite	1.72–1.75	Rose quartz	1.544–1.553		
Spinel	1.712–1.762	Smoky quartz	1.54–1.55		
Kyanite	1.710–1.734	Andesine	1.543–1.557		
Vesuvianite	1.70–1.72	Iolite (Cordierite)	1.542–1.578		
Diaspore	1.69–1.75	Jasper	1.54		
Tanzanite	1.691–1.700	Amber	1.539–1.545		
Phosphosiderite	1.69–1.74	Ivory	1.535–1.570		
Dumortierite	1.678–1.723	Pearls	1.53–1.69		
Axinite	1.674–1.704	Aragonite	1.525–1.685		
Hypersthene	1.673–1.731	Lepidolite	1.53–1.556		
Diopside	1.66–1.72	Agate	1.53–1.54		
Kornerupine	1.660–1.699	Chalcedony	1.53–1.54		
Hiddenite	1.660–1.681	Chrysoprase	1.53–1.54		
Kunzite	1.660–1.681	Amazonite	1.514–1.539		
Sillimanite	1.657–1.680	Sunstone	1.525 1.548		
Malachite	1.655–1.909	Unakite	1.52–1.76		
Jadeite	1.652–1.688	Ammolite	1.52–1.68		
Peridot	1.650–1.703	Maw–sit–sit	1.52–1.74		
Enstatite	1.66–1.75	Moonstone	1.518–1.532		
Phenakite	1.650–1.670	Magnesite	1.515–1.717		
Apatite	1.63–1.655	Lapis lazuli	1.50		
Jeremejevite	1.630–1.653	Tugtupite	1.496–1.502		

Gemstones in the Order of their Descending Density (Specific Gravity)

Platinum (pure)	21.4	Malachite	3.25–4.10	Lapis Lazuli	2.50–3.00
Gold (pure)	19.3	Enstatite	3.2–3.5	Howlite	2.45–2.71
Silver (pure)	10.49	Tanzanite	3.2–3.4	Serpentine	2.44–2.62
Cuprite	6.00–6.15	Diopside	3.2–3.4	Variscite	2.42–2.58
Scheelite	5.90–6.12	Gaspéite	3.21–3.70	Haüyne	2.4–2.5
Sugilite	5.5–6.5	Apatite	3.16–3.23	Tugtupite	2.36–2.57
Zircon	5.5–5.9	Hiddenite	3.15–2.21	Obsidian	2.35–2.50
Hematite	5.00–5.28	Kunzite	3.15–2.21	Moldavite	2.32–2.38
Pyrite	4.85–5.10	Sillimanite	3.14–3.25	Turquoise	2.31–2.84
Marcasite	4.85–4.92	Andalusite	3.13–3.23	Sodalite	2.15–2.30
YAG	4.55	Amblygonite	2.98–3.06	Hackmanite	2.15–2.35
Psilomelane	4.4–4.72	Fluorite	3.00–3.25	Opal	1.98–2.50
Spessartine	4.1–4.2	Magnesite	3.00–3.12	Chrysocolla	1.90–2.45
Smithsonite	4.3–4.65	Danburite	2.97–3.03	Ivory	1.70–2.0
Ruby	3.97–4.05	Phenakite	2.95–2.97	Jet	1.19–1.35
Sapphire	3.95–4.03	Brazilianite	2.94–3.00	Amber	1.05–1.09
Zircon	3.93–4.73	Aragonite	2.93–2.97		
Almandine	3.8–4.25	Nephrite	2.9–3.03		
Sphalerite	3.9–4.1	Tourmaline	2.82–3.32		
Rhodolite	3.85	Prehnite	2.8–2.95		
Pyrope	3.7–3.8	Lepidolite	2.8–3.3		
Uvarovite	3.7–3.81	Ammolite	2.75–2.84		
Demantoid	3.7–4.1	Larimar	2.75–2.90		
Melanite	3.7–4.1	Sugilite	2.69–2.79		
Azurite	3.70–3.89	Aquamarine	2.68–2.80		
Chrysoberyl	3.7–3.78	Emerald	2.67–2.80		
Hessonite	3.64–3.69	Red beryl	2.66–2.70		
Benitoite	3.61–3.69	Labradorite	2.65–2.75		
Taaffeite	3.6–3.62	Andesine	2.65–2.69		
Tsavorite	3.57–3.73	Amethyst	2.65		
Spinel	3.54–3.63	Citrine	2.65		
Kyanite	3.53–3.70	Onyx	2.65		
Phosphosiderite	3.5–4.0	Rock crystal	2.65		
Rhodonite	3.50–3.76	Rose quartz	2.65		
Diamond	3.50–3.53	Aventurine	2.64–2.69		
Topaz	3.49–3.57	Sunstone	2.62–2.65		
Grossular	3.4–3.8	Pearl	2.6–2.85		
Rhodochrosite	3.4–3.7	Coral	2.60–2.70		
Sphene (titanite)	3.4–3.6	Agate	2.60–2.64		
Hypersthene	3.4–3.5	Pietersite	2.6		
Vesuvianite	3.3–3.5	Jasper	2.58–2.91		
Epidote	3.3–3.5	Calcite	2.58–2.75		
Hemimorphite	3.3–3.5	Iolite (Cordierite)	2.58–2.66		
Diaspore	3.3–3.5	Moonstone	2.54–2.63		
Jadeite	3.30–3.38	Amazonite	2.56–2.58		
Peridot	3.28–3.48	Unakite	2.55–3.20		
Kornerupine	3.28–3.35	Seraphinite	2.55–2.75		
Dumortierite	3.26–3.41	Charoite	2.54–2.78		
Axinite	3.26–3.36	Maw–sit–sit	2.5–3.2		

Bibliography

Books & Booklets

Anderson, B. W. *Gem Testing*. Verplanck, NY: Emerson Books, 1985.

Arem, Joel. *Color Encyclopedia of Gemstones*. New York: Chapman & Hall, 1987.

Bauer, Jaroslav & Bouska, Vladimir. *Pierres Precieuses et Pierres Fines*. Paris: Bordas, 1985.

Bauer, Dr. Max. *Precious Stones Volume II*. New York: Dover Publications: 1968, English translation first published in 1904.

Bonewitz, Ronald. *Rock & Gem*. New York: Dorling Kindersley Ltd., 2008.

Butler, Gail, *Crystal & Gemstone Divination*. Baldwin Park, CA: Gem Guides Book Co, 2008.

CIBJO *Gemstone Book*, Bern, Switzerland. World Jewellery Confederation, 2010.

Cornejo, Carlos & Barorelli, Andrea. *Minerals & Precious Stones of Brazil*. Sau Paulo: Solaris Cultural Publications, 2009.

Crowe, Judith. *The Jeweler's Directory of Gemstones*. Buffalo, NY: Firefly Books, 2006.

Deer, W. A., Howie. R. A., Zussman, J. *An Introduction to the Rock-Forming Minerals: Second Edition*. Essex, England: Longman Scientific & Technical, 1992.

Eason, Cassandra. *The Illustrated Directory of Healing Crystals*. London: Collins & Brown, 2004.
ExtraLapis, *Calcite No.4*. East Hampton, CT: Lithographic, LLC, 2003.
ExtraLapis, *Fluorite: The Collector's Choice*. East Hampton, CT: Lithographic, LLC. 2006.
ExtraLapis, *Smithosonite No 13*. East Hampton, CT: Lithographic, LLC. 2010.

Gemological Institute of America. *Gem Reference Guide*. Santa Monica, CA: GIA, 1988.

Grande, Lance, & August, Allison. *Gems & Gemstones*. Chicago: Univ. of Chicago Press, 2009.

Gubelin, Eduard J. *The Color Treasury of Gemstones*. New York: Thomas Y. Crowell, 1984.

Gubelin, Eduard J. & Koivula, John I. *Photoatlas of Inclusions in Gemstones, Volume 3*. Basel: Opinio Publishers, 2008.
Gubelin, Eduard J. & Koivula, John I. *Photoatlas of Inclusions in Gemstones, Volume 2*. Basel: Opinio Publishers, 2005.
Gubelin, Eduard J. & Koivula, John I. *Photoatlas of Inclusions in Gemstones*. Zurich: ABC Edition, 1986.

Hall, Cally. *Eyewitness Handbooks, Gemstones*. London: Dorling Kindersley, 1994.

HRD, *Gemmology Basic Course*. Antwerp: HRD, 2005.

Hurlbut, Cornelius. *Dana's Manual of Mineralogy*. New York: John Wiley & Sons, 1971.
Hurrell, Karen & Johnson, Mary L. *Gemstones*. New York: Metro Books, 2008.

Kunz, George Frederick. *The Curious Lore of Precious Stones*. New York: Bell, 1989.
Kunz, George Frederick. *Gems & Precious Stones of North America*. New York: Dover, 1968.

Lapis International. *Calcite the Mineral With the Most Forms #4.* East Hampton, CT: Lapis International. LLC, 2003.

Liddicoat, Richard T. *Handbook of Gem Identification.* Santa Monica, CA: GIA, 1989.

Lithographic, LLC. *Smithsonite: Think Zinc #13.* Denver: Lithographic, LLC, 2010.
Lithographic, LLC. *Fluorite: The Collector's Choice.* Denver: Lithographic, LLC, 2006.

Nassau, Kurt. *Gemstone Enhancement, Second Edition.* London: Butterworths, 1994.

Newman, Renée. *Exotic Gems: Volume 2.* Los Angeles: Intl. Jewelry Publ., 2011.
Newman, Renée. *Exotic Gems: Volume 1.* Los Angeles: Intl. Jewelry Publ., 2010.
Newman, Renée. *Gemstone Buying Guide.* Los Angeles: Intl. Jewelry Publications, 2008.

O'Donoghue, Michael, Joyner Louise. *Identification of Gemstones.* Oxford, Butterworth Heinemann, 2003.
O'Donoghue, Michael. *Synthetic, Imitation & Treated Gemstones.* Oxford: Butterworth-Heinemann, 1997.

Polk, Patti. *Collecting Rocks, Gems & Minerals.* Iola, WI: Krause Publications, 2010.

Pough, Frederick. *Peterson Field Guides, Rocks and Minerals.* Boston: Houghton Miffln, 1983.

Read, Peter G. *Gemmology.* Oxford: Butterworth-Heineman, 1996.

Rubin, Howard. *Grading & Pricing with GemDialogue.* New York: GemDialogue Co., 1986.

Russell, Henry. *Encyclopedia of Rocks, Mineral & Gemstones.* London: Brown Partworks Ltd., 2001.
Schumann, Walter. *Gemstones of the World.* New York: Sterling, 1997.

Sinkankas, John. *Van Nostrand's Standard Catalogue of Gems.* New York: Van Nostrand Reinhold, 1968.
Sinkankas, John. *Gemstone & Mineral Data Book.* Prescott, AZ. Geoscience Press, 1988.

Sofianides, Anna & Harlow, George. *Gems & Crystals from the American Museum of Natural History.* New York: Simon & Shuster, 1990.

Thomas, Arthur. *The Gemstones Handbook.* UK: New Holland Publishers, 2008.

Wallis, Keith. *Gemstones: Understanding, Identifying, Buying.* Woodbridge, England: Antique Collector's Club, 2011.

Webster, Robert. *Gemmologists' Compendium.* New York: Van Nostrand Reinhold, 1979.
Webster, Robert. *Gems, Fourth Edition.* London, Butterworths,1983.
Webster, Robert. *Practical Gemmology.* Ipswich, Suffolk: N. A. G. Press, 1976.

White, John S. *The Smithsonian Treasury Minerals and Gems.* Washington D.C.: Smithsonian Institution Press, 1991.

Wise, Richard. *Secrets of the Gem Trade.* Lenox, MA: Brunswick House Press, 2003.

Zeitner, June Culp, *Gem & Lapidary Materials.* Tucson, AZ: Geoscience Press, 1996.

Periodicals

Auction Market Resource for Gems & Jewelry. P. O. Box 7683 Rego Park, NY, 11374.
Australian Gemmologist. Brisbane: Gemmological Association of Australia.
Canadian Gemmologist. Toronto: Canadian Gemmological Association.
Gem & Jewellery News. London: Gemmological Association and Gem Testing Laboratory of Great Britain.
Gems and Gemology. Santa Monica, CA: Gemological Institute of America.

The GemGuide. Glenview, IL: Gemworld International, Inc.

InColor: New York: ICA (International Colored Gemstone Association).

Jewellery Business. Richmond Hill, ON: Kenilworth Media, Inc.

Jewelers Circular Keystone. Radnor, PA: Chilton Publishing Co.

JQ Magazine. San Francisco: GQ Publishing.

Jewelry News Asia. Hong Kong: CMP Asia Ltd.

Jewellery Review. Hong Kong: Brilliant Art Group.

Journal of Gemmology, London: Gemmological Association & Gem Testing Laboratory of Great Britain.

Lapidary Journal Jewelry Artist. Loveland, CO: Interweave Press.

Mineralogical Record. Tucson, AZ: Mineralogical Record, Inc.

National Jeweler. New York: National Business Media.

Palmieri's Auction/FMV Monitor. New York, NY: GCAL

Rock & Gem. Ventura, CA: Miller Magazines, Inc.

Rocks & Minerals. Philadelphia: Taylor and Francis Group.

Southern Jewelry News. Greensboro, NC: *Southern Jewelry News*.

Miscellaneous: Courses

Gem A Diploma in Gemmology Course, 2009.

Gemological Institute of America Gem Identification Course.

Gemological Institute of America Gem Identification Lab Manual.

Gemological Institute of America Colored Stone Grading Course.

Gemological Institute of America Colored Stones Course.

Informational Websites Used for This Book

www.galleries.com

www.geminterest.com

www.gemologyonline.com

www.gemstonemagnetism.com

www.irocks.com

www.jtv.com

www.palagems.com

www.palaminerals.com

www.mindat.org

www.minerals.net

www.rarestone.com

www.webmineral.com

Index

Other Books by RENÉE NEWMAN
Graduate Gemologist (GIA)

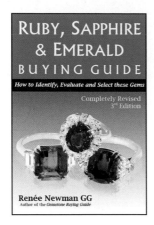

Ruby, Sapphire & Emerald Buying Guide
How to Identify, Evaluate & Select these Gems

An advanced, full-color guide to identifying and evaluating rubies, sapphires and emeralds including information on treatments, grading systems, geographic sources, fakes, synthetics, lab reports, appraisals, and gem care.

"**Enjoyable reading . . . profusely illustrated with color photographs** showing not only the beauty of finished jewelry but close-ups and magnification of details such as finish, flaws and fakes . . . Sophisticated enough for professionals to use . . . highly recommended . . . **Newman's guides are the ones to take along when shopping**."
Library Journal

"**Solid, informative and comprehensive** . . . dissects each aspect of ruby and sapphire value in detail . . . a wealth of grading information . . . a definite thumbs-up!"
C. R. Beesley, President, American Gemological Laboratories, *JCK Magazine*

187 pages, 280 photos, 267 in color, 6" by 9", ISBN 978-0929975-41-2, US$19.95

Pearl Buying Guide
How to Evaluate, Identify, Select and Care for Pearls & Pearl Jewelry

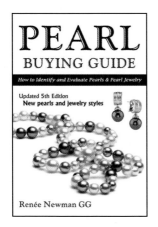

"**Copious color photographs** . . . explains how to appraise and distinguish among all varieties of pearls . . . takes potential buyers and collectors through the ins and outs of the pearl world."
Publisher's Weekly

"**An indispensable guide** to judging [pearl] characteristics, distinguishing genuine from imitation, and making wise choices . . . useful to all types of readers, from the professional jeweler to the average patron . . . **highly recommended**."
Library Journal

"A **well written, beautifully illustrated** book designed to help retail customers, jewelry designers, and store buyers make informed buying decisions about the various types of pearls and pearl jewelry."
Gems & Gemology

154 pages, 321 photos (207 are new), 6" by 9", ISBN 978-0929975-44-3, US$19.95

Exotic Gems, Volume 2

How to Identify and Buy Alexandrite, Andalusite, Chrysoberyl Cat's-eye, Kyanite, Common Opal, Fire Opal, Dinosaur Gembone, Tsavorite, Rhodolite & Other Garnets

"The subtitle of this book says is all: . . . Not familiar with some of these stones? Your jewelry designs might be missing out. Like its predecessor, *Exotic Gems, Volume 1*, this handy guide helps you find, evaluate, buy and care for these stones with plenty of photos of finished jewelry."

Bead & Button, reviewed by StacyWerkheis

"The best thing about this series is the focus - Newman manages to include enough information and photographs from the likes of John Koivula interspersed with fun facts, metaphysical properties, history and ancient lore and so many photos that everyone from Gemologists to Jewelry Lovers will relate, understand and treasure these books. . . My favorite thing about these books is that Newman is not afraid to cover many of the opaque gems that have so long been overlooked as well as sourcing the latest, newest, and the sometimes controversial, gems in the field. Thanks for another winner Renee!"

"A Fly on the Wall Views & Reviews," reviewed by Robyn Hawk

"Renee Newman never disappoints us, does she? She has written another outstanding book about gemstones that we can learn from, teach from, and recommend to our clients . . . I do think that this book will serve appraisers well."

The Jewelry Appraiser, reviewed by Kim Piracci

". . . those familiar with Newman's previous books will recognise the in depth, yet understandable style, catering to professionals and lay people alike . . . Chapter nine on common opal is a real eye opener, Newman deftly capturing the beauty found in an assortment of colours including Peruvian pink, Andean blue, green, yellow and even lime through excellent and abundant photographs. Interesting issues about classification and the term 'fire' are discussed in the chapter on fire opal. Opal treatments are analysed in depth.

The remainder of the book is devoted to the complex group of garnets about which gemmologists and mineralogists disagree when defining species and varieties. Gemmologists will find the technical information in this section most valuable. In the fascinating pages of photographs, we are shown how a master cutter cuts a garnet. The 'horsetail' inclusions in demantoid garnets, unlike inclusions in most other garnets, are desirable. We are also directed to publications offering more detailed information.

Imparting a wealth of information on gemstone evaluation, as usual, with tips on detecting imitations, synthetics and gem treatments, Newman always entertains with interesting anecdotes of history, geographic sources and metaphysical lore of gems. Be ready to be informed and entertained. Didn't know what the 'alexandrite effect' was or what comprises the interesting crew digging up Arizona garnets? You will now."

The Australian Gemmologist, reviewed by Carol Resnick

154 pages, 408 color photos, 6" x 9", ISBN 978-0-929975-42-9, US$19.95

For more information, see **www.reneenewman.com**

Other Books by RENÉE NEWMAN

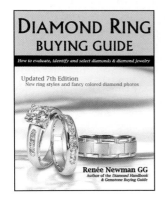

Diamond Ring Buying Guide
How to Evaluate, Identify and Select Diamonds & Diamond Jewelry

"**An entire course on judging diamonds in 156 pages of well-organized information**. The photos are excellent . . . Clear and concise, it serves as a check-list for the purchase and mounting of a diamond . . . another fine update in a series of books that are useful to both the jewelry industry and consumers."

Gems & Gemology

"**A wealth of information** . . . delves into the intricacies of shape, carat weight, color, clarity, setting style, and cut—happily avoiding all industry jargon and keeping explanations streamlined enough so even the first-time diamond buyer can confidently choose a gem."

Booklist

"Succinctly written in a step-by-step, outlined format with plenty of photographs to illustrate the salient points; it could help keep a lot of people out of trouble. Essentially, it is a **fact-filled text devoid of a lot of technical mumbo-jumbo.** This is a definite thumbs up!"

C. R. Beesley, President, American Gemological Laboratories

15 pages, 274 color & b/w photos, 7" X 9", ISBN 978-0-929975-40-5, US$18.95

Gem & Jewelry Pocket Guide
Small enough to use while shopping locally or abroad

"**Brilliantly planned, painstakingly researched, and beautifully produced** . . . this handy little book comes closer to covering all of the important bases than any similar guides have managed to do. From good descriptions of the most popular gem materials (plus gold and platinum), to jewelry craftsmanship, treatments, gem sources, appraisals, documentation, and even information about U.S. customs for foreign travelers—it is all here. I heartily endorse this wonderful pocket guide."

John S. White, former Curator of Gems & Minerals at the Smithsonian *Lapidary Journal*

"**Short guides don't come better than this**. . . . As always with this author, the presentation is immaculate and each opening displays high-class pictures of gemstones and jewellery."
Journal of Gemmology

154 pages, 108 color photos, 4½" by 7", ISBN 978-0929975-30-6, US$11.95

Available at major bookstores and jewelry supply stores
For more information, see **www.reneenewman.com**

Exotic Gems, Volume 1

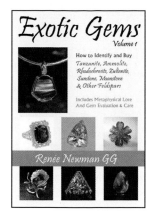

This is the first in a series of books that explores the history, lore, evaluation, geographic sources, and identifying properties of lesser-known gems. *Exotic Gems, Volume 1* has detailed info and close-up color photos of mounted and loose tanzanite, labradorite, zultanite, rhodochrosite, sunstone, moonstone, ammolite, spectrolite, amazonite andesine, bytownite, orthoclase and oligoclase.

"Chapters including 'Price factors in a nutshell' will prove indispensable to novice buyers. The breadth of information on each stone, Renee's guide to choosing an appraiser, 288 vibrant photos and a bibliography also make this book a handy resource for seasoned collectors. We'll be watching for future installments of the *Exotic Gems* series." *Bead & Button*

". . . contains many many color photographs that cover the spectrum of subjects from mining locality shots to cutting to subtle color variations to the finished jewelry, as appropriate . . . A quick glance at the acknowledgments shows that a great deal of networking and editorial effort has gone into this book. If you want to buy one of the materials covered by this book, already have spent your money but want an appraisal, or are just plain interested in zultanite, I highly recommend *Exotic Gems Volume 1.*" *Rocks & Minerals*

154 pages, 288 color photos, 6" x 9", ISBN 978-0-929975-42-9, US$19.95

Jewelry Handbook
How to Select, Wear & Care for Jewelry

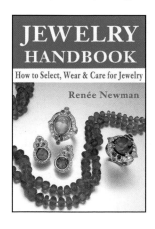

The *Jewelry Handbook* is like a Jewelry 101 course on the fundamentals of jewelry metals, settings, finishes, necklaces, chains, clasps, bracelets, rings, earrings, brooches, pins, clips, manufacturing methods and jewelry selection and care. It outlines the benefits and drawbacks of the various setting styles, mountings, chains, and metals such as gold, silver, platinum, palladium, titanium, stainless steel and tungsten. It also provides info and color photos on gemstones and fineness marks and helps you select versatile, durable jewelry that flatters your features.

"**A great introduction to jewellery** and should be required reading for all in the industry." Dr. Jack Ogden, CEO Gem-A (British Gemmological Association)

"**A user-friendly, beautifully illustrated guide,** allowing for quick reference to specific topics." *The Jewelry Appraiser*

"**Valuable advice for consumers and the trade**, specifically those in retail sales and perhaps even more for jewelry appraisers . . . An easy read and easy to find valuable lists and details." Richard Drucker GG, *Gem Market News*

177 pages, 297 color & 47 b/w photos, 6" x 9", ISBN 978-0-929975-38-2, US$19.95

Other Books by RENÉE NEWMAN

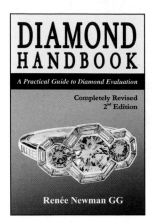

Diamond Handbook
A Practical Guide to Diamond Evaluation

Updates professionals on new developments in the diamond industry and provides advanced information on diamond grading, treatments, synthetic diamonds, fluorescence, and fancy colored diamonds. It also covers topics not in the *Diamond Ring Buying Guide* such as diamond grading reports, light performance, branded diamonds, diamond recutting, and antique diamond cuts and jewelry.

"Impressively comprehensive. . . . a practical, well-organized and concisely written volume, packed with valuable information. The *Diamond Handbook* is destined to become an indispensable reference for the consumer and trade professional alike."
Canadian Gemmologist

"The text covers everything the buyer needs to know, with useful comments on lighting and first-class images. No other text in current circulation discusses recutting and its possible effects ... **This is a must for anyone buying, testing or valuing a polished diamond and for students in many fields.**" *Journal of Gemmology*

186 pages, 320 photos (most in color), 6" x 9", ISBN 978-0-929975-39-9, US$19.95

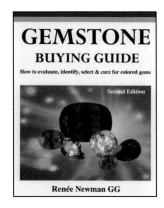

Gemstone Buying Guide
How to Evaluate, Identify and Select Colored Gems

"Praiseworthy, **a beautiful gem-pictorial reference** and a help to everyone in viewing colored stones as a gemologist or gem dealer would.... One of the finest collections of gem photographs I've ever seen ... If you see the book, you will probably purchase it on the spot."
Anglic Gemcutter

"A quality Buying Guide that is recommended for purchase to consumers, gemmologists and students of gemmology—irrespective of their standard of knowledge of gemmology. The information is comprehensive, factual, and well presented. Particularly noteworthy in this book are the quality colour photographs that have been carefully chosen to illustrate the text. *Australian Gemmologist*

"Beautifully produced. .... With colour on almost every opening few could resist this book whether or not they were in the gem and jewellery trade."
Journal of Gemmology

154 pages, 281 color photos, 7" X 9", ISBN 978-0929975-34-4, US$19.95

Order Form

TITLE	Price	Quantity	Total
Rare Gemstones	$19.95		
Exotic Gems, Volume 2	$19.95		
Exotic Gems, Volume 1	$19.95		
Ruby, Sapphire & Emerald Buying Guide	$19.95		
Gemstone Buying Guide	$19.95		
Diamond Handbook	$19.95		
Pearl Buying Guide	$19.95		
Jewelry Handbook	$19.95		
Diamond Ring Buying Guide	$18.95		
Gem & Jewelry Pocket Guide	$11.95		
Osteoporosis Prevention	$15.95		
Book Total			
SALES TAX for California residents only **(book total x $.0825)**			
SHIPPING: USA: first book $4.00, each additional copy $2.00 Canada & Mexico - airmail: first book $11.00, ea. addl. $5.00 All other foreign countries - airmail: first book $14.00, ea. addl. $7.00			
TOTAL AMOUNT with tax (if applicable) and shipping (Pay foreign orders with an international money order or a check drawn on a U.S. bank.) **TOTAL**			

Available at major book stores or by mail. For quantity orders e-mail:
intljpubl@aol.com

Mail check or money order in U.S. funds

To: International Jewelry Publications
P.O. Box 13384
Los Angeles, CA 90013-0384 USA

Ship to:

Name_____

Address_____

City_____ State or Province_____

Postal or Zip Code_____ Country _____

Osteoporosis Prevention

" . . . a complete, practical, and easy-to-read reference for osteoporosis prevention** . . . As the founding president of the Taiwan Osteoporosis Association, I am delighted to recommend this book to you."
                    Dr. Ko-En Huang, Founding President of TOA

"The author, Renée Newman has abundant experience in translating technical terms into everyday English. She writes this book about osteoporosis prevention from a patient's perspective. These two elements contribute to **an easy-to-read and understandable book for the public. To the medical professions, this is also a very valuable reference.**"
          Dr. Chyi-Her Lin, Dean of Medical College, Natl Cheng
                              Kung Univ / Taiwan

"I was impressed with the comprehensive nature of *Osteoporosis Prevention* and its use of scientific sources. . . .The fact that the author has struggled with bone loss and can talk from personal experience makes the book more interesting and easy to read. Another good feature is that the book has informative illustrations and tables, which help clarify important points. I congratulate the author for writing **a sound and thorough guide to osteoporosis prevention.**"   Ronald Lawrence MD, PhD
          Co-chair of the first Symposium on Osteoporosis of the National Institute on Aging

" . . . **clarifies the inaccurate concepts from the Internet**. It contains abundant information and really deserves my recommendation."
              Dr. Yung-Kuei Soong, The 6th President of Taiwanese Osteoporosis Association

"The book is written from a patient's experience and her secrets to bone care. This book is **so interesting that I finished reading it the following day** . . . The author translates all the technical terms into everyday English which makes this book so easy to read and understand."
                    Dr. Sheng-Mou Hou, Ex-minister, Dept. of Health / Taiwan

"**A competent and thoroughly 'reader friendly' approach to preventing osteoporosis.** Inclusive of information on how to: help prevent osteoporosis and broken bones; get enough calcium and other bone nutrients from food; make exercise safe and fun; retain a youthful posture; select a bone density center; get maximum benefit from your bone density exam; understand bone density reports; help seniors maintain their muscles and their bones; and how to be a savvy patient. *Osteoporosis Prevention* should be a part of every community health center and public library Health & Medicine reference collection . . ."
                                        Midwest Book Review

"With great interest, I have read Renée Newman's *Osteoporosis Prevention* which provides complete and practical information about osteoporosis from a patient's perspective. . . . **a must-read reference for osteoporosis prevention.**"
Dr. Tzay-Shing Yang, 3rd President of TOA, President of Taiwan Menopause Care Society

You can get free information about osteoporosis prevention, bone density testing and reports at: **www.avoidboneloss.com**

176 pages, 6" X 9", ISBN 978-0929975-37-5, US$15.95